REBELS
AND
REVOLUTIONARIES
VOICES OF AMERICAN LABOR

REBELS AND REVOLUTIONARIES

VOICES OF AMERICAN LABOR

Nancy Whitelaw

MORGAN
REYNOLDS

PUBLISHING

Greensboro, North Carolina

Social Critics and Reformers

REBELS AND REVOLUTIONARIES:
VOICES OF AMERICAN LABOR

Copyright © 2007 by Nancy Whitelaw

Library of Congress Cataloging-in-Publication Data

Whitelaw, Nancy.
  Rebels and revolutionaries : voices of American labor / by Nancy
Whitelaw.
      p. cm. -- (American workers)
  Includes bibliographical references and index.
  ISBN-13: 978-1-59935-037-0
  ISBN-10: 1-59935-037-8
  1. Socialists--United States--Biography. 2. Socialism--United States--
Biography. 3. Labor movement--United States--Biography. 4. Social reform-
ers--United States--Biography. I. Title.
  HX84.A2W45 2007
  335.0092'273--dc22
  [B]
                                              2007007558

Printed in the United States of America
First Edition

To Ruth Bannister—
You are an inspiration to me in many ways—most of all
for the ways you care about and love people

Contents

Eugene V. Debs
(Library of Congress)

one

Eugene Debs:

"You're the greatest power between the earth and stars"

During the second half of the nineteenth century, many of the citizens of Terre Haute, Indiana, believed the end of the world was near and that the Kingdom of God was at hand. This belief in the imminent end of the world created a sense of urgency. It was important that everyone be ready. The local school board tried to insure that the young people would maintain a moral life by insisting on strict obedience, good manners, and respect for adults, all within the framework of Christianity.

It was in this town that Eugene Victor Debs was born on November 5th, in 1855. As a teenager, Eugene believed he knew an easy formula for success. It would require him to do two things—live a moral life and work hard. The moral life was easy: the community he grew up in fostered morality. Debs called his birthplace the "beloved little community of Terre Haute, where all were neighbors and friends."

And for Debs, working hard was part of living a moral life. Eugene started working for his father, Jean Daniel Debs, an immigrant from Alsace, a province in eastern France, in the family grocery store.

Eugene was not interested in games, spending time with friends, or going to church. He preferred working in the store, selling solid butter at a dime a pound, chickens for a dime each, and string beans for a nickel a quart. After work, he liked to listen as his father read aloud from the French classics.

He learned much of his history from his father's reading: he learned of the French Enlightenment from the writings of Voltaire and Rousseau, and he heard from the great German writers Goethe and Schiller. Indeed, Jean Daniel Debs had named his son for two nineteenth-century writers and social reformers, Victor Hugo and Eugene Sue, and he and his wife, Marguerite, also spoke French and German to their six children.

Eugene was third among his four sisters and younger brother. Six feet tall, long-legged, and wiry, he quit school at age fourteen and took a job scraping grease and paint off locomotives at the local Vandalia Railroad yards for fifty cents. At night, he attended classes at a local business college.

By 1871, he had moved up to locomotive fireman, a job that consisted of shoveling coal into the engine. During the winter, one side of his body would feel the biting cold and the other side would be drenched in sweat from the blazing engine heat. It was a tough job, but in keeping with his attitude toward hard work and morality. He was a good, willing worker, confident that he would rise through the ranks and become a highly paid and respected engineer or conductor.

Terre Haute was a railroad town, and a good job on the railroad would make Eugene one of its respected citizens.

Then the depression of 1873 struck. Debs, along with thousands of other workers, lost his job. He briefly found railroad work again in St. Louis, Missouri, but his mother worried that her son might get injured—or worse—doing hazardous railway work. She convinced him to return home, and he took a job as a billing clerk at Hulman & Cox, a wholesale grocer.

Although no longer connected to the railroad industry, Debs remained friendly with railroad workers, and he developed an interest in the connection between business and politics. He signed up as a charter member of the Brotherhood of Locomotive Firemen in 1875 and became its recording secretary.

The Brotherhood had originally been founded to fight for insurance and funeral benefits for its members. Railroad work was considered so dangerous that insurance companies would not issue policies to workers.

Over time, the Brotherhood took up other causes, evolving into one of the first railroad unions. At first, its leadership focused on encouraging workers to provide managers and owners of the railroad with the assistance they needed to make the railroad more profitable, the rationale being that this would raise the economic status of everyone. But workers became increasingly impatient at how long it was taking for the profits to trickle down to them, and they began demanding better pay and working conditions. Wages for railroad workers had dropped 23 percent between 1873 and 1876, and another 10 percent by May 1877.

In June 1877, the Pennsylvania Railroad announced yet another 10 percent cut. Labor leaders blamed the decrease in wages on a kickback to selected corporate shippers. The lowered wages led to a series of strikes around the state, and those strikes quickly spread to cities across the country. Some of the strikes turned violent, and President Rutherford B. Hayes sent federal troops into West Virginia and Maryland to quell revolts against management there.

Terre Haute workers began their strike on July 23, and five days later soldiers of the Third U.S. Infantry received orders to open the depot. As the troops approached, the strikers surrendered. After a promise that no retaliation would be taken against them and that employers would consider a wage increase, the strikers returned to work.

Debs opposed the strike, advocating instead cooperation and arbitration over confrontation. He recognized the tendency of employers to consider the interests of corporate executives over those of workers, but he believed that it was possible to influence owners to "enter upon a more righteous code of conduct," as well as encourage employees to be "worthy of confidence and respect." Writing in a railroad workers' magazine, he asked: "Does the Brotherhood encourage strikers? To this question we must emphatically answer, No, brothers."

Although he distanced himself from the strike, Debs remained a tireless organizer for the Brotherhood. He enjoyed immersing himself in organizational details, and eventually he came to believe that a well-coordinated strike could be a valuable tool.

In the years following the strike of 1877, employers began blacklisting strikers. Coupled with a nationwide economic depression, this blacklisting decimated union membership. Some displaced union members looked to politicians for aid. They found support in the Greenback Party and the Independent Party.

THE GREAT STRIKE—BLOCKADE OF ENGINES AT MARTINSBURG, WEST VIRGINIA.—From Photograph by D. Bendann.—[See Page 626.]

THE GREAT STRIKE—BURNING OF THE LEBANON VALLEY RAILROAD BRIDGE BY THE RIOTERS.—Drawn by Fred. B. Schell.—[See Page 626.]

Pictures from the August 11, 1877, issue of *Harper's Weekly* depicting the strike in West Virginia *(Library of Congress)*

Debs rejected both these parties, claiming they were too interested in their own concerns and didn't care about the good of the community. He declared his support for the Democratic Party. He believed the Democrats, like himself, believed in getting along with others peacefully and did not distinguish between the social classes, as both employees and employers were members of the Democratic Party.

In 1879, he sought election as city clerk in Terre Haute. He won against ten competitors, thanks to support from Republicans and Democrats, laborers and upper-class voters alike. His time in office was not without controversy. He refused, for example, to set fines for prostitutes. Why should the women be punished, he reasoned, when their male customers were allowed to get away scot-free? Despite the controversy, Debs was reelected to the position in 1881. He also became editor of *The Locomotive Firemen's Magazine* in 1880, as well as secretary-treasurer of the Brotherhood.

Then in 1884, Debs ran for the Indiana state assembly on a Democratic platform that advocated reduction in work hours for state employees, establishment of a Bureau of Labor, and an end to child labor. People liked his plain speaking, his knowledge of workers' lives, and his ordinary dress of overalls and a railroader's cap. He campaigned in railroad yards and in neighborhoods, and easily won.

One of Debs's first acts as legislator was to draft a bill requiring railroad companies to compensate workers for injuries suffered on the job, but the bill was defeated before it came to a vote. He also could not find support for other issues, such as suffrage for women or the abolition of distinctions of race and color in state laws. Debs decided that he was not suited for the compromise and favoritism of a political life and decided not to run for reelection.

The year after serving a term in the Indiana legislature he met Kate Metzel, the stepdaughter of a prominent drugstore owner in Terre Haute. On June 9, 1885, a few months before his thirtieth birthday, they wed at St. Stephen's Episcopal Church. Five years later Debs built his wife, whom he called "Ducky," a house for $4,500. The couple remained together for the rest of Debs life and did not have children.

Debs helped found the Occidental Literary Club of Terre Haute, a weekly debating club, and became its first president. Debs brought in the most prominent, nationally known speakers of the time, such as Susan B. Anthony, the women's rights crusader; Col. Robert G. Ingersoll, a champion of freethinking who became known as "the great agnostic;" Wendell Phillips, a radical abolitionist and defender of rights for American Indians and women; and James Whitcomb Riley, a popular children's poet who was also reportedly a drinking buddy of Debs's.

Debs credited the literary club with helping hone his speaking skills. He gave his first speech before the membership on his hero, Patrick Henry, but he later recalled a "keen sense of humiliation and shame" about the experience, as well as "big drops of cold sweat standing out all over me." Afterwards, Debs made a conscious decision to educate himself on vital issues. "I bought an encyclopedia on the installment plan, one volume each month, and began to read and study history and literature and to devote myself to grammar and composition." His growing skill as an orator and organizer would serve him well as he got more involved with politics and labor unions.

During the last decades of the nineteenth century, when Debs was at his prime, labor organizations in the United

States saw a steady rise in membership, as more and more people migrated from rural to urban areas. It was the norm for women and children to work eleven- to twelve-hour days, six and seven days a week. Benefits such as vacation or sick days, disability pay, or unemployment compensation were nonexistent. Moreover, wages were low and working conditions dangerous.

Labor organizations, such as the Knights of Labor, began fighting for eight-hour days, fair pay, and an end to child labor. The Knights of Labor, founded in 1869 under the leadership of Terence V. Powderly, was perhaps the first national labor organization with local chapters throughout the United States. Its membership was open to any worker, regardless of race, gender, or skill. Only lawyers, bankers, gamblers, and liquor dealers were not allowed to join, and the organization favored arbitration over strikes.

The Knights of Labor's rival, the American Federation of Labor (AFL) was an organization of craft, or trade, unions. Founded in 1886 by a cigar maker named Samuel Gompers, the AFL advocated better wages and working conditions for its members as well. But the AFL did not permit unskilled laborers to join. It was open to skilled white men, many of whom worked on the railroads as car builders, machinists, and repairmen. Most notably, unlike the Knights of Labor and the Brotherhood of Locomotive Firemen, the AFL used strikes and boycotts to force management to the bargaining table.

Remaining active with the Brotherhood, Debs traveled throughout the East, organizing railroad workers, carpenters, printers, and other laborers. He was popular and charismatic, able to hold crowds' attention with stories and jokes. Debs became serious, though, when he talked about the need for workers to accept their duties and responsibilities and to maintain moral honor.

Anti-union feelings were strong within government and big business, and they worked to discredit unions and strikers. Meanwhile, rifts developed between different types of railroad workers. The Brotherhood of Local Firemen (BLF), for example, adopted a platform that forbade members to attend the annual convention of locomotive engineers. Conflict within the unions also arose over the issue of strikes. Some wanted the option of going out on strike as a final resort when the railroad managers refused to negotiate with them. Others feared strikes would make it easy for the union to be labeled as radical and un-American. This issue came to a head for the Brotherhood in 1885 when they deleted the no-strike clause from their constitution.

Debs worked to smooth over the conflict over the strike clause and to generally promote a spirit of solidarity among the workers. Despite his best efforts, the strike issue remained divisive. Many were ready to strike and impose boycotts to force a change in management practices, while others supported a general reform of the economy.

Debs favored the latter approach: he believed that only a broad-based reform of the political and economic system could permanently improve worker's lives. He wanted to create a strong federation of railroad workers and spent time with different chapters of the Brotherhood, urging them to organize. His first priority was not to create strike situations. He insisted the stronger federation of railroad workers was needed "not for the purpose of fostering or encouraging strikes, but to avert them."

With the election of 1892 approaching, Debs turned to politics. He believed business interests controlled the Republican presidential candidate, Benjamin Harrison. Democratic candidate Grover Cleveland, however, had shown respect for workers' rights. Debs supported Cleveland, who won the close election.

Meanwhile, Debs began to develop a plan to unite railroad workers into one collective bargaining unit, and this union would be modeled after the U.S. Constitution. The separate organizations, made up of different railway jobs, would be treated like states in a union. This plan recognized the distinctive problems and needs of workers in different job classifications, as well as the issues that were of concern to them all. The American Railway Union (ARU) was formed on June 20, 1893, and Debs was named its first president. He appealed to his fellow organizers to allow black as well as white workers to join the new union. However, the idea was shot down. Only white workers, with the exception of those in management, were permitted to join.

That same year, a deep economic depression gripped the nation, after a run on the New York stock market. As the business crisis grew, close to five hundred banks and more than 15,000 businesses went bankrupt. Thousands of others were threatened with failure, including railroad companies. In a frantic attempt to cut production costs, companies slashed wages and fired workers. Soon thousands were without jobs, and the number of hungry and homeless people grew every day. Suddenly there was a renewed interest in alternative economic systems such as communism and socialism. Both philosophies believed in government control of the essential industries. Communists usually advocated a violent seizure of power, while many Socialists were willing to try to change the economic system through the political process.

Those who managed to keep their jobs discovered that management was increasingly resistant to cooperating with their workers. The federal government usually came down on the side of the owners and managers and intervened in a number of cases with injunctions that forced workers to accept management demands.

James Hill, owner/manager of the Great Northern Railway, slashed wages in 1893 and again in 1894. His workers, most of whom had recently joined Debs's newly formed American Railroad Union, threatened a strike unless management agreed to meet with them. Management, however, refused to recognize the union as a legal entity or negotiate with it. On April 13, the strike began, and Great Northern Railway superintendents were ordered to fire any worker they believed was sympathetic to the union.

Debs, as president of the union, countered that members were required by their union regulations to strike when management refused to talk. He even spoke to the Chamber of Commerce, a group expected to be anti-worker. At the end of his talk, the Chamber demanded that the dispute be submitted to arbitration between the union leaders and management. The arbitration resulted in workers receiving almost all of their demands. The new American Railway Union had won its first strike, but there were more battles to come.

In Chicago, the Pullman Palace Car Company, which built expensive passenger railroad cars, slashed the wages of its hourly workers by 25 percent. But there was no reduction in the salaries of officers, managers, or supervisors. George Pullman, the company's founder, also raised the rents for workers who lived in the houses he owned near the company. Pullman had built a town in his name, south of Chicago, where many of his workers rented homes. With the simultaneous lowering of wages and raising of rates, 3,000 workers went on strike in retaliation.

Although Debs initially did not support the decision, the American Railway Union voted to boycott the Pullman Company. They decided to try to stop any train with a Pullman car from moving. Debs sent instructions to every lodge not to use violence. He also warned them not to stop any trains carrying the mail. If the mail did not move, the federal government would have a reason to intervene and break up the strike.

The strike spread day-by-day as more workers left their jobs, and more trains stopped running. In just one day, 125,000 workers joined the boycott, tying up more than twenty railroad lines. Debs talked to as many groups of workers as he could, urging them to have courage and commitment to their cause.

Soon the strike spread beyond the Pullman Company and began to hurt other railroad companies as well. Workers in more than twenty states and territories eventually launched their own strikes as a show of support for their Pullman brothers.

The owners reacted by forming their own organization and began to pressure President Cleveland's administration to stop the strike. The owners made several arguments against the strike, but the most powerful, as Debs had feared, was that the strike was interfering with the delivery of the U.S. mail.

The U.S. Attorney-General Richard Olney, whose sympathies were with the owners, declared that the national railroad strike was illegal on the grounds that it interfered with mail delivery. Furthermore, he declared that because the strike had interfered with several railroads, it constituted an illegal trust as established in the recently passed Sherman antitrust law. Although the Sherman Act was designed to limit the monopoly power of the giant trusts, Olney used it against the union. He issued an injunction for the strikers to cease and had the injunction delivered directly to Debs. This was a warning to Debs that he would be held personally responsible if the strike continued.

Richard Olney *(Library of Congress)*

If the strike stopped, all the sacrifices of the workers would have been for nothing. Such a defeat would probably be the end of the American Railway Union. The union board voted to ignore the injunction. Debs knew he was at legal risk and hired Clarence Darrow, one of the most successful attorneys of the day, to defend him.

To back up the federal injunction against the strike, U.S. president Grover Cleveland ordered thousands of federal troops to Chicago. As the soldiers gathered and waited, ready to enforce the decrees of the federal courts, Debs announced, "The first shots fired by the regular soldiers at the mobs here will be the signal for a civil war."

The presence of federal troops in Chicago infuriated many of the strikers. On July 5, 1894, fires broke out near a park, and the next day a mob, many members of which were not strikers or members of the ARU, set fire to several railway cars. The flames spread, and several hundred cars were destroyed. The mob violence continued the next day, and in the end, more than thirty workers lost their lives.

The violence played right into the owners' hands, and Debs knew it. He pleaded with the strikers, "I appeal to you to be men, orderly and law-abiding. Our cause is just, the great public is with us, and we have nothing to fear."

As the violence continued, it undercut public support for the strike. President Cleveland declared martial law in the Chicago area and on July 10, Debs was arrested on the charge of conspiracy to interfere with interstate commerce. He asked to meet with company officials to offer the compromise that strikers would stop the boycott if the company would agree to rehire the strikers who were ARU members, but the officials refused to see him.

The strike collapsed. Any strikers allowed to return to their jobs were forced to sign contracts in which they pledged not to join a union. Debs was imprisoned in Cook County Jail on July 17, in a cell with five other inmates. He eventually persuaded prison officials to bring a fox terrier into the cell to kill the giant rats that scurried around in the dark.

When he was finally released on bail, Debs testified at government investigations of the boycott. In his testimony he declared that there would be no need for labor unions if employers dealt honorably with workers. He insisted that a strike is justified in the face of tyranny, regardless of the consequences.

The final report of the government investigation commission was actually favorable to the ARU. It stated that the blame for the boycott "rests with the people themselves and with the government for not adequately controlling monopolies and corporations, and for failing to reasonably protect the rights of labor and redress its wrongs."

Meanwhile, the failure of the strike and boycott created divisions within the American Railroad Union. When Debs criticized the union for missing other opportunities to fight for labor, the conflict with the union grew nasty. When other leaders accused Debs of being a dictator and claimed he was a drunkard and racketeer, he resigned.

Surveying the wreckage of the failed Pullman Strike, Debs was certain of one thing: both the Republican and Democratic parties had failed to protect the rights of workers. He declared: "I am a Populist, and I favor wiping out both old parties . . . go to the polls and vote the People's ticket." He went on further to say the economic depression was created by big business and bankers.

On January 7, 1895, Debs appeared late for his trial on conspiracy charges in Woodstock. He was wearing a well-tailored suit with a boutonniere and looked and sounded like a minister or business executive as he gave the excuse that he had been ill with indigestion. Rumors circulated that he was drunk. At the conclusion of the trial, Debs was sentenced to three months in jail for obstruction of mails and interference with interstate commerce.

In the McHenry County jail, Debs organized prisoners. They elected officers, gave themselves the name of Co-operative Colony of Liberty Jail, drilled, and studied economics and history. He communicated with hundreds of supporters on the outside and even wrote a weekly article for the Chicago *Evening Press* and frequently gave interviews to reporters.

Debs spent much of his time in jail reading and studying about socialism. One of the books that had the most influence over him was *Das Kapital* by Karl Marx. *Das Kapital* laid out the foundation for the Marxist-Communist philosophy that became the dominant anti-capitalist ideology in the twentieth century. Debs later wrote that it was during his months in jail that he became a socialist.

Debs was released on November 22, 1895. Ten thousand supporters came to cheer his release. The festive atmosphere did not extend to the American Railroad Union headquarters and the labor union world at large. Membership was down and the movement was divided into two camps. One group aligned with Samuel Gompers, whose American Federation of Labor wanted to take a more conciliatory policy toward corporations. The other group was more hostile toward corporations and wanted a political solution to the problems between owners and workers.

This latter group turned to Debs, whom they already respected for his actions, devotion to the cause, charisma, and leadership. Although Debs had decided that socialism was the answer to the problems plaguing American workers, he was not yet ready to publicly commit to socialism. During the 1896 election he supported the nominee of the Democratic Party, William Jennings Bryan. Republican William McKinley won the general election in a landslide.

Debs was now ready to go make public his break with the two-party system. On January 1, 1897, he announced that he had turned to socialism: "The issue is Socialism versus Capitalism. I am for Socialism because I am for humanity."

Debs traveled all over the country to speak and build support for socialism. He rode in dirty trains, ate greasy food, and seldom saw his wife. Although he had recently been a prisoner, local officials usually greeted him with respect and praised him for his support of decent wages and improved working conditions.

Debs's new party, the Social Democratic Party of the United States, opened a national office on October 1, 1898. Debs was a member of the executive board and treasurer, as well as one of the principle writers for the party's weekly newspaper, the *Social Democratic Herald*.

Debs accepted the nomination of the Social Democrats to run for president in 1900 against Republican William McKinley and Democrat William Jennings Bryan. McKinley won the election, with Bryan a close second and Debs a distant third.

After the defeat, Debs continued to travel and speak throughout the country. When he spoke, he paced back and forth across the platform and sometimes knelt with his arms outstretched. In warm months, sweat dripped from his chin and forehead, and his shirt would be soaked by the end of a speech. Many of those who heard him speak remembered it with awe. "He is a true disciple of Jesus Christ," he "has a great soul," and "I love him," they said.

In 1901, the Social Democrats merged with other small parties and formed the Socialist Party. In 1904, 183 delegates of the Socialist Party met for their second national convention in Chicago. Again, Debs was asked to be the nominee for president. He initially refused but was persuaded to enter the race.

In the November election, Debs received 420,000 votes, losing to Republican Theodore Roosevelt, who had become

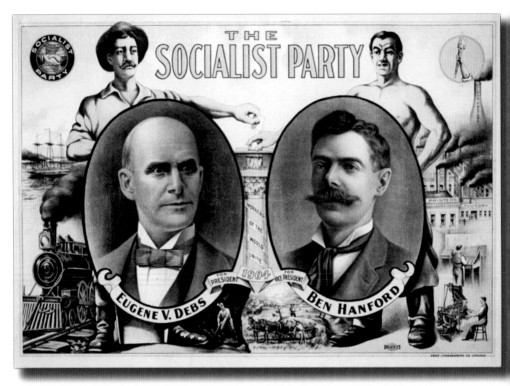

In 1904, Debs campaigned as the Socialist Party's presidential nominee.
(Library of Congress)

president after McKinley was assassinated in 1901, and Democrat Judge Alton Parker.

Exhausted and frequently defeated, Debs did not lose sight of his vision. He became more committed to ending the capitalist system and declared publicly that the objective of the workingman should be to overthrow the current economic system. "The end of class struggles and class rule, of master and slave, of ignorance and vice, of poverty and shame, of cruelty and crime—birth of freedom, the dawn of brotherhood, the beginning of MAN. . . . This is socialism."

Debs also participated in the founding of a new organization named Industrial Workers of the World (IWW), which shared many of his goals of creating a unified party for all workers, as opposed to separate unions for each industry. He said, "As individual wage-slaves, you are helpless and your condition hopeless. As a class, you are the greatest power between the earth and the stars." But when the IWW became more committed to a violent overthrow of the U.S. government, Debs resigned his membership.

Debs decided to stop speaking before racially segregated audiences. He was convinced that racial and religious conflict was harmful to the workers' cause. In the *International Socialist Review*, he wrote that prejudiced whites were "ignorant, lazy, unclean, totally devoid of ambition, themselves the foul products of the capitalist system."

At the Socialist Party's national convention of 1908, the delegates again voted for nominees to run against William Jennings Bryan, again the Democratic nominee, and Republican William Howard Taft. Debs received 90 percent of the vote.

The Socialist Party came up with creative methods to draw attention to their campaign. One was a tent camp where farmers and their families met for vacations and enjoyed square dancing, revival meetings, and were encouraged to join the party. Another innovation was a locomotive and sleeping car, dubbed "Red Special," that carried Debs and his entourage around the country on a speaking tour. Thousands met the Red Special as it chugged through Illinois, Iowa, Nebraska, Colorado, and the West Coast.

As the campaign wore on, it was apparent that Debs was exhausted. It seemed that his voice would not hold out. When he returned to Chicago, he had set a record of speaking to 275,000 people on a journey that covered

15,000 miles. He then left Chicago for New York City, where he spoke to crowds of 10,000 at a time.

The final election tally gave Debs 420,000 votes, about the same total that he had received in 1904. Taft was elected President.

After the campaign, Debs suffered from severe exhaustion and perpetual headaches. He rested much of the spring and summer of 1909 before setting off on another journey crisscrossing the country, speaking to as many people as would listen.

As the presidential campaign of 1912 neared, Debs resolved to run for president again. "I think the outlook is positively inspiring . . . the gods are all with us," he said.

A variety of political buttons from Debs's many presidential campaigns
(Courtesy of Corbis)

At the national Socialist Party convention he received three-fifths of the ballots on the first vote. Theodore Roosevelt, who had left the Republican Party, was running for president on the Bull Moose ticket. Taft was the Republican candidate again, and New Jersey governor Woodrow Wilson was the Democratic candidate. Although a world war was impending in Europe, none of the candidates focused on foreign policy. Debs received 900,000 votes, but Wilson won.

Debs qualified his stance against violent conflict on the part of union members when militia was sent to Ludlow, Colorado, to break up a strike of miners. When the militia turned machine guns on the strikers and their families, Debs urged retaliation. "You should have no more compunction in killing them [militia] than if they were so many mad dogs or rattlesnakes that menaced your homes and your community . . . when a law fails . . . then an appeal to force is not only morally justified, but becomes a patriotic duty" he said.

In August of 1914, war broke out in Europe. Debs blamed the bloody conflict on the greed of capitalists. He spent months traveling the country speaking against the war and warning that America must not get involved. "Any nation that today prepares for war incites war and slaughter," he insisted. Although some members of the Socialist Party supported a U.S. program of war preparedness, Debs continued to speak out against American involvement throughout the winter and spring of 1916.

Debs rejected all new attempts to draft him to run for president in 1916. He was a Socialist candidate for U.S. Congress in the Fifth Congressional District of Indiana. His message was socialism against capitalism. In two weeks during September, he traveled over the district in his Model T touring car and gave fifty-five speeches. When the Republican candidate won an easy victory, Debs consoled himself and his supporters by reminding them he had been true to his ideals throughout the campaign.

On April 6, 1917, the United States declared war on Germany and the other axis powers. After an emergency meeting, the Socialist Party declared its opposition to the war.

Thousands of other Americans protested against United States involvement in the war. In response, an espionage law was interpreted so to justify imprisonment of anyone who spoke against the war. Antiwar publications were banned, and vigilantes terrorized those who stood up against the conflict.

When the government crack down on war resisters continued, Debs called for a national campaign to insure the civil rights of all citizens.

A photograph of Debs giving a speech from the back of a train

On June 16, 1917, after a fiery speech that lasted more than two hours, Debs was arrested on charges of conspiracy against the war. He stayed in jail overnight and was freed on bond the next day. That same day he was nominated to run for Congress by Socialists in Terre Haute, the group that had paid his bond. He explained that he would not be a free man for very long and could not run for Congress. Despite some severe attacks of painful lumbago, Debs made speeches during the summer, supporting the nominee who replaced him, a glassmaker named Shubert Sebree.

In early September, Debs was tried for making "criminal" statements in his speeches. His lawyers answered that his arrest and trial was a violation of his First Amendment rights and he should be acquitted. Debs was his own final witness at the trial: he admitted he was opposed to the present form of government in America and compared himself to George Washington, Samuel Adams, and Patrick Henry. He said there could be no such thing as brotherhood when workers had to fight one another for jobs, and business and professional men had to fight one another for trade. He concluded by saying that it was not he, but institutions in the United States, that should be on trial. Reportedly, some members of the jury were weeping when he finished speaking.

The next day, the judge instructed the jury to find the defendant not guilty of the counts of ridiculing the government. He left open the question of whether he was guilty of obstruction of the conscription act, which allowed the government to draft men into the army to fight the war. The jury returned the verdict of guilty on three counts. Debs spoke again before he was sentenced the next day.

Debs in prison

It was assumed by most of the audience that liquor had loosened his tongue. He spoke grandly of his kinship with and sympathy for the downtrodden. After his speech he was sentenced to ten years in prison. His lawyers immediately started an appeal to the Supreme Court.

The war ended while Debs was still in Terre Haute awaiting the outcome of the Supreme Court decision. In March 1919, the U.S. Supreme Court upheld his conviction, and sixty-four-year-old Eugene Debs entered the Moundsville Federal Prison in West Virginia.

While Debs served his sentence, his prison cell door was never locked and he could wander freely in the prison yard. He spent most of his time reading and chatting with other inmates and visitors. Two months later he was moved to the federal prison in Atlanta, Georgia, where his health suffered from confinement in a hot and airless cell fifteen hours a day and from wretched food. He also had chronic lumbago, heart trouble, and blinding headaches.

While in prison, Debs was able to receive newspapers. He learned that the Socialist Party split into two smaller and less effective parties. One group wanted unity with the more militant Third Communist International; the other group opposed this move toward a more violent strategy. This split weakened the Socialist Party and essentially destroyed its effectiveness. Debs wrote and urged all Socialists to recognize their common goals.

A Socialist national convention selected Debs as their presidential candidate in 1920 to run against Republican Warren Harding and Democrat James Cox. Asked how he could carry on a campaign from prison, Debs laughed and said, "I will be a candidate at home in seclusion. It will be much less tiresome and my managers and opponents can always locate me." A round, red campaign button, with Debs's image on it, urged voters to cast their presidential ballot for "Convict # 9653."

In the 1920 election, Harding won by an overwhelming margin. Debs summed up his feelings: "In my mature years, I no longer permit myself to be either disappointed or discouraged . . . the people can have anything they want. The trouble is they do not want anything."

On January 19, 1921, before the beginning of Harding's term, Attorney General Palmer asked President Wilson to consider commuting Debs's sentence because he was sixty-five and in poor health. When the president refused to grant him the release, Debs replied, "It is he [Wilson], not I, who needs a pardon."

World War I ended officially with a peace treaty in November 1921. The following Christmas Day, Debs, along with twenty-three other political prisoners, was released from prison. As Debs's train pulled into the Terre Haute station, a cheering crowd of more than 25,000 people met him as fire bells chimed and celebratory torches swung in the wind.

Debs at his desk (*Library of Congress*)

Prison had taken a severe toll on his health. His stomach and kidneys no longer functioned properly. Recurrent headaches had become even more of a problem, and rheumatism and lumbago twisted his muscles. His erratic heartbeat and raspy breathing kept him awake nights.

Despite pleas from those around him to allow him to rest, Debs was besieged with letters, telegrams, visitors, and requests. The Socialist Party had abandoned much of its campaign for industrial unionism, so Debs focused on the urgent need to reform conditions in prisons. He was contracted to write a series of twelve articles about prisons for the Bell Syndicate, which published newspapers all over the country. However, he broke his agreement not to insert any political propaganda into the articles. Nine articles were published after some editing, and the other three were not printed at all.

In his last years, Debs refused to take part or give support to any political party. He wrote to a party leader: "You cannot seem to understand that I am sick and worn and that I have not had the ghost of a chance to rest since I got out of the penitentiary." He finally agreed to a doctor's warning that he must go to a sanitarium for a complete rest for several months. When his health had recovered somewhat, he occasionally sneaked away from the health facility with friends to enjoy a meal.

In November 1923, Debs returned to Terre Haute, but by December he was again confined to bed. This time he never fully recovered. Throughout the spring and summer, he spoke as often as his strength would allow, but he was often overcome by nervous exhaustion. He returned home.

He was still confined to bed in the spring of 1924, and realized that the end was near. He donated most of his library to the Rand School of Social Science. He did write, with some optimism: "Socialism will never die. It is inevitable. We may retard or impede its progress through our political organization. But the inevitable cannot die."

Bad health forced him back to the sanitarium, where he took some treatments and, again, broke the regulations by leaving for restaurant dinners with his friends, allowing his room to fill with visitors and frequently wandering away from the facility. In the 1924 presidential election, he unequivocally supported the Socialist-endorsed candidate Robert LaFollette, who lost to Republican Calvin Coolidge.

His wife Kate also suffered from poor health. The couple traveled to Bermuda in March 1925 for a complete rest. Unfortunately, the return trip on rough seas brought on extreme seasickness.

On October 15, 1926, Debs lapsed into a coma following a heart attack and died on October 20 at Lindlahr Sanitarium in Elmhurst, Illinois. His death brought on an outpouring of grief throughout the country. Many memorial meetings were held in large cities and small villages. Fellow socialist Norman Thomas addressed a crowd from Debs's front porch at the funeral.

Looking back on his life as an old man, Debs remembered how he became committed to working to improve the lives of American workers. While working on a railroad, he recalled, his vision for himself changed from one of concentration on personal goals to one of concern for workers everywhere:

> [A]s a locomotive fireman, I learned of the hardships of the rail in snow, sleep, and hail, of the ceaseless danger that lurks

along the iron highway, the uncertainty of employment, scant wages, and altogether trying lot of the working man, so that from my very boyhood I was made to feel the wrongs of labor.

Despite seemingly overwhelming obstacles and setbacks, Eugene Debs remained true to what he believed, and many of his suggested reforms have become a part of the American way of life. Even today, Americans are benefiting from his influence on the country.

EUGENE DEBS
— timeline —

1885 Born on November 5 in Terre Haute, Indiana.

1867 Quits school at age fourteen to take job at local railroad yard.

1875 Becomes a charter member of the Brotherhood of Locomotive firemen.

1879 Elected to first of two terms as city clerk in Terre Haute.

1884 Elected to Indiana General Assembly as a Democrat.

1885 Marries Kate Metzel, stepdaughter of a prominent drug store owner in Terre Haute.

1893 Forms the American Railway Union; the new union wins its first strike.

1894 American Railway Union goes on strike against Pullman Palace Car Company; jailed after strike fails.

1897 Announces his break with two-party system; advocates socialism.

1900 Runs for U.S. president as candidate of Social Democratic Party of the United States against William McKinley; McKinley wins.

1904 Runs for president again, as candidate for the newly formed Socialist Party; loses to Theodore Roosevelt.

1908 Makes third bid for office of the president as Socialist Party candidate against William Howard Taft; loses election.

1912 Runs for president against Republican Theodore Roosevelt and Democrat Woodrow Wilson; Wilson wins.

1916 Defeated in run for Congress in Indiana.

1918 Arrested on charges of conspiracy after making fiery antiwar speech protesting World War I in Europe; sentenced to ten years in prison after jury delivers a guilty verdict on three counts.

1919 Begins serving prison sentence.

1920 Makes his fifth bid for president, urging voters to cast their ballot for "Convict #9653"; Republican Warren Harding wins.

1921 Released for Christmas; welcomed home by crowd of more than 25,000.

1925 Travels with wife to Bermuda for rest.

1926 Dies on October 20 at Lindlahr Sanitarium in Elmhurst, Illinois.

Emma Goldman
(Library of Congress)

MOTHER EARTH

Vol. VII. · JUNE, 1912 No. 4

SAN DIEGO EDITION

two
Emma Goldman:

"I have my one Great Love—my Ideal"

E
mma Goldman was a rebel from the day she was
born in Kovno, Russia, on June 27, 1869. As a child
it was her hot-tempered father, Abraham Goldman,
whom she rebelled against. Emma wrote in her memoir, "As
long as I could think back, I remembered his saying that he
had not wanted me." Her mother, Taube, on the other hand,
was an educated woman whom Emma admired for her ability to think for herself and for her political activism.

Although Emma had two stepsisters and two brothers,
she remembered her childhood as lonely at best, chaotic at
worst. Her parents frequently quarreled, and Emma learned
to distrust the adults around her.

Life was difficult for most Russians, as it had been for
generations. Rich nobles owned all the land, and poor, frequently illiterate servants called serfs farmed for them. Until
1861, the serfs were legal slaves that could be bought and

PATRIOTISM IN ACTION

sold by their owners. In 1861, a law set the serfs free, but because they had no money or education most were not able to get jobs. Most freed serfs remained on the farms where they were before freedom and continued to live and to labor as their ancestors had done for centuries.

The czars, rulers of Russia, were often tyrants with little concern for their subjects' welfare. The society and laws were riddled with privileges and exceptions for the aristocracy. Peasants were mistreated because they were peasants; Jews were beaten because they were Jews; females were scorned because they were females.

Jews faced special prejudice in Russia. They were forced either to convert to Christianity or to live in designated ghettoes, many in a Black Sea area officially known as the Pale of Settlement. Their choices of occupation and education were restricted, they were forced to wear clothes quickly identifying their religion, and the building of synagogues was strictly regulated. These discriminatory regulations and brutal poverty kept Jews, such as Emma Goldman's family, in a constant battle to survive.

While Emma was a child, the prejudice against Jews frequently became violent. In riots called pogroms, armed Russian Cossacks swept into Jewish ghettos on horses, looting and killing. Jews who could not hide when the "Pogrom!" alarm was sounded were slaughtered. Many who did hide emerged to find that their houses were destroyed and their property stolen.

Emma saw cruelty all around her. Abraham was an innkeeper, and many of the inn's guests were at their worst—drinking too much, bragging about their treatment of serfs, beating women and children, abusing animals, and fighting each other. Emma's father was frustrated at how he had to earn his living. He became increasingly short-tempered and often took out his frustration by berating Emma and sometimes beating her. Despite this ill treatment, Emma remained loyal to him.

Emma could be difficult in her own way. She refused to behave either at school or at home. Then she met a teacher whom she loved and who gave her respect and attention. Under this woman's guidance, Emma decided to reform her behavior and work toward becoming a doctor—despite the fact that Jews were restricted from practicing medicine in Russia. She passed the admission test for high school, but when a teacher there read her elementary discipline record she was refused admission.

On March 1, 1881, Czar Alexander II was assassinated. The conspirators hoped his killing would set off a widespread popular revolution and that the peasants, students, and other downtrodden Russians would rise up. They miscalculated. The new czar, Alexander III, turned out to be far more oppressive than his predecessor. Inevitably, Jews were blamed for the assassination, more anti-Jewish legislation was enacted, and government leaders encouraged pogroms.

With some family help, Abraham was able to open a store, while Emma attended school. There she began to study the revolutionary movement in Russia. She thought the revolutionaries were admirable heroes and martyrs and dreamed that she too would risk her life if she saw the need and opportunity. Emma began to develop a vision of peace and justice for all Russians. Because people were responsible for the injustice in the world, she reasoned that only the people could eliminate injustice.

Abraham tried in vain to beat the rebelliousness out of his petite daughter. After Emma started working in a corset factory, she began to sneak around with a new group of revolutionary friends. Abraham became enraged when he discovered she had been to gatherings where boys and girls met together, and beat her severely. Emma resolved to get away from her father and, as soon as she could, travel to the United States, a country that welcomed refugees.

Abraham tried to head off her plan to emigrate by completing marriage arrangements for her. When fifteen-year-old Emma insisted she needed to finish school before marriage, her father burned her books, saying, "Girls do not have to learn much. All a Jewish daughter needs to know is how to prepare minced fish, cut noodles fine, and give the man plenty of children."

Emma's married sister, Lena, already lived in Rochester, in upstate New York, and her sister Helena had decided to emigrate as well. Determined to join her sisters, Emma told her father if he did not let her go, she would drown herself. Abraham believed her and reluctantly let her go.

In December 1885, she and Helena boarded the steamship *Elbe* bound for the United States. When they arrived in New York Harbor, the sight of the Statue of Liberty thrilled Emma and Helena. "Ah, there she was, the symbol of hope, of freedom, of opportunity!" Emma later recalled. "She had her torch high to light the way to the free country, the asylum for the oppressed of all lands. We, too, Helena and I, would find a place in the generous heart of America. Our spirits were high, our eyes filled with tears."

Almost immediately after disembarking from the boat, disillusionment set in. The sisters were met by the "gruff voices" of immigration officials who "roughly pushed us, hither and thither, shouted orders to get ready." Emma questioned whether she had replaced a life of misery in Russia with the same in America. Eventually, the young idealist and her sister made their way to Lena's place.

Their new neighborhood was much like a ghetto in Russia. Immigrants, especially Jews, were scorned because of their heavy accents, and employment opportunities were limited. Immigrants were streaming into the country, more than five million in the 1880s and almost four million more in the 1890s. Most offered to work for little pay.

Cheap labor was a major reason why businesses were so profitable in the late nineteenth and early twentieth centuries. The discrepancy in wages between workers and management was wide to begin with and steadily increased. American labor activists tried unsuccessfully to organize immigrant laborers, but they were too overwhelmed with adjusting to the new land and exhausted by ten- to sixteen-hour workdays to focus on building a union.

Goldman eventually found a job in a factory that made overcoats. The factory overseers forbade employees to sing or talk or even go to the bathroom without permission. Goldman almost broke under the strain of working more than ten hours a day. Her weekly salary as a seamstress of $2.50 was hardly enough to pay for food. When she was refused a raise, she quit her job.

Goldman decided to join a local German Socialist club where the members talked about a society in which the government helped people to achieve a fair standard of living. The group was small, unlike the large Socialist organizations that existed in the big cities, such as New York and

Chicago, where a labor movement was growing. Around the 1900s, the numbers of immigrants willing and able to listen to the promises of labor leaders increased. Unions such as the National Labor Union, the Knights of Labor, and the American Federation of Labor tried to improve working conditions.

Goldman met a fellow worker and Jewish immigrant from Russia, Jacob A. Kersner, who asked her to marry him about four months after their first meeting. She feared that she would lose her independence if she married, but decided to take a chance and accepted his proposal.

Her fears proved portentous. They married in February 1887 and after the wedding, Kersner stopped her from working, causing her to lose the little bit of money that was her own. She was bored—home alone all day while Kersner worked and all night while he played cards.

Meanwhile, Chicago had become a hotbed of labor activism and radical thought, and in May 1886 a violent conflict between the police and workers broke out there. News of the riot in Haymarket Square shook Goldman. The incident began with a rally of strikers demonstrating for an eight-hour workday. Several political groups, some advocating an overthrow of the United States government, attended the meeting. In the evening, after a long day of speeches and marches, a bomb was thrown into the crowd. The bomb exploded and killed some police officers and workers.

Blame for the bomb was quickly placed on the anarchists, although there was no proof of their involvement. Newspapers and other publications, such as the *Albany Law Journal*, echoed majority opinion when it editorialized that the lives of good citizens were "at the mercy of a few long-haired wild-eyed,

A photograph of anarchists and labor demonstrators in Union Square
(*Library of Congress*)

bad-smelling, atheistic, reckless foreign wretches, who never did an honest hour's work in their lives."

At a trial for the bombing, eight anarchists and union leaders were convicted of conspiracy to murder, although no evidence was presented to prove their guilt. Four were sentenced to jail terms and four were hanged.

Goldman became enraged at what she saw as the injustice of the arrests and executions—she even attacked a woman she heard speak in favor of the convictions. "With one leap I was at the woman's throat," Goldman recalled. When she was in control of herself, she resolved once again to spend the rest of her life working for justice and equality, and for a peaceful society free of interference from a government dedicated to supporting the powerful at the expense of the majority. "I had a distinct sensation that something new and wonderful had been born in my soul," she remembered.

Goldman became an anarchist at a time when citizens in Italy, Russia, and Spain, as well as in the United States, were uniting to declare their commitment to an ideal system of justice. Some of the new thinkers were Socialists, some Communists, and some anarchists.

Socialists advocated government control of the economy and believed laws and regulations could establish this. Communists advocated a cooperative society similar to the Socialists, but most Communist leaders were ready to use force to overthrow the existing government and to make sure the new one lived up to its ideals. Anarchists advocated destruction of all centralized authority and thought all governments, regardless of their intentions, inevitably became the tool of the few used to oppress the many. Anarchists believed that a bloody revolution by the people would be necessary.

Anarchy appealed to Goldman for many reasons. As a student in St. Petersburg she had been sympathetic to students who took part in the revolution. Growing up in Russia, she was well aware of the atrocities a government could inflict on the poor and weak, and her work experience in the United States had shown her how the poor suffered under unchecked capitalism. She believed that the key to true liberation lay in rejection of authoritarian values. Her first personal step into her new life as an anarchist was to divorce Kersner. Her parents, who had moved to the United States in the fall of 1886, and everyone else in her family, except for Helena, disowned her for this scandalous act.

Twenty-year-old Goldman left Rochester and lived briefly in New Haven, Connecticut, where she worked at a corset factory, before finally settling in New York City.

She arrived in New York with only a sewing machine, $5.00, and the hope that she could get help from her fellow anarchists and revolutionaries. She soon met Alexander (Sasha) Berkman, who invited her to a small hall to hear Johann Most speak. Most was the editor of the German-language paper *Freiheit,* which encouraged social revolution through violent protest. Goldman accepted Berkman's invitation to see Most, and she was introduced to the newspaper editor.

Sasha Berkman *(Library of Congress)*

In time, Goldman came to deeply admire, even idolize, Most. He also became her mentor and lover. She assisted him with work at the newspaper office and he, in turn, organized her first public speaking tour, which included stops in Rochester, Buffalo, and Cleveland. She described the first time she publicly spoke: "something strange happened. . . . Words I had never heard myself utter before came pouring forth, faster and faster." When she finished the applause was overwhelming. This marked the start of a long career as a public speaker.

Goldman also began working as an organizer for the anarchist movement. She arranged meetings, led demonstrations, distributed leaflets, and lectured, sometimes in German and Yiddish.

She also became Berkman's lover. They rented a four-room apartment and shared space with Berkman's cousin and one of their mutual friends. The four lived communally, each giving all he or she had to the group and taking only what was needed.

While Goldman, Berkman, and their compatriots worked to fund a trip to Russia to promote international anarchy, they heard about a strike that had erupted in Homestead, Pennsylvania. Steel workers at the giant Carnegie Steel Company were demanding better wages and working conditions. Henry Frick, the plant manager of Carnegie Steel, was determined to end the strike without meeting the demands of the strikers. During negotiations, he announced that management would no longer talk with workers and that the plant would immediately become nonunion. Then on July 6, 1892, Frick hired guards who killed nine steel workers.

Henry Frick *(Library of Congress)*

Suddenly, instead of a fight for better wages, the dispute had become a fight for the right to organize. Goldman was thrilled: "It sounded the awakening of the American worker, the long-awaited day of his resurrection." She and her comrades decided they could be more useful in Homestead than in Russia.

As the strike turned bloody, Goldman and her friends plotted to assassinate Frick. "Frick was the symbol of wealth and power, of the injustice and wrong of the capitalistic class, as well as personally responsible for the shedding of the workers' blood," Goldman later recalled. "Sasha's act would be directed against Frick, not as a man, but as the enemy of labour." Goldman and her comrades also realized that it was likely that the assassination would end in death for the killer as well as for Frick. Berkman was eager to become the martyr.

They pooled their money and found they had $15.00, enough to pay for Berkman's trip to Pennsylvania with a dollar left for one day's food and lodging. They needed $20.00 more to get him a gun and clothes suitable for getting into Frick's office without arousing suspicion. To raise the money, Goldman borrowed $5.00 and began working as a prostitute. She got the idea from Sonya, a character in one of her favorite books, *Crime and Punishment.* Sonya had prostituted herself to make money for her little brother and sister, and Goldman reasoned that her cause was far greater. Although the thought of prostituting revolted her, Goldman talked herself into it, saying, "Sasha is giving his life and you shrink from giving your body, miserable coward!" She made the needed money.

In Homestead on July 23, 1892, Berkman dressed in his new suit and put a gun in one pocket and a dagger in another. He pinned a dynamite capsule in his lapel lining. He talked his way into Frick's office by posing as a man who could help Frick replace the fired strikers. Inside the office, he fired twice at Frick's head and then managed to stab Frick in the leg three times before guards wrestled him to the ground.

Although the wounds were severe, Frick recovered and the attack became a propaganda victory for the anti-union cause. The Homestead plant soon reopened with nonunion labor. Accused of attempted murder, Berkman refused to hire a lawyer because he did not believe in the legal system. He was sentenced to twenty-two years in prison.

The failed assassination created a fear of anarchy throughout the country, and more Americans refused to accept revolution or to even join a union. Most people believed the right to hold office and the right to vote were sufficient tools to change the government when it needed changing. When newspaper reports linked Goldman to Berkman, she was labeled as a dangerous anarchist and went into hiding.

Goldman met regularly with fellow anarchists to find a way to get Berkman's sentence commuted. At one such meeting, she met Edward Brady, an Austrian who had just arrived in the United States after spending ten years in a prison for publication of illegal anarchist literature. The two developed what she called a "beautiful comaradery." They read French together, he cooked meals in her apartment for her and her roommates, and he supported her efforts to free Berkman. Goldman and Brady addressed rallies and distributed food to the unemployed, and in time, they also became lovers. At a demonstration of more than 4,000 people at Union Square in New York City, Goldman advised: "Demonstrate before the palaces of the rich, demand work. If they do not give you work, demand bread. If they deny you both, take bread. It is your sacred right!"

Meanwhile, a stock market panic in 1893 turned into a deep economic depression, resulting in a major loss of jobs. Anarchists seized this opportunity to seek new members.

They promised that in an anarchist society there would be no unemployment.

Goldman gained both supporters and opponents with her frank defense of atheism, free speech, homosexuality, and sexual freedom. The growing list of people who criticized Goldman included some who worked with her and found her personality domineering and her impatience with opposition overly hostile.

Goldman became known as "Red Emma" and was often arrested. She was convicted for inciting violence and sentenced to one year in Blackwell's Island Penitentiary on the East River in New York City. Although conditions were difficult in the prison, she was allowed to read volume after volume of history and philosophy. She concluded: "The State of New York could have rendered me no greater service than by sending me to Blackwell's Island Penitentiary." She said her time there only strengthened her political ideals and determination.

When Goldman left prison in August of 1894, she supported herself by working as a nurse, and a few months after her release she moved in with Brady. She spent all her free time lecturing against capitalism and launched a new campaign to secure Berkman's release.

In August 1895, she left the United States for Europe, stopping first in England and then Scotland, where she addressed large crowds. She reached her final destination, Vienna, in October. There, she studied to get a nursing degree so she could earn more money.

In the course of a year in Vienna, Goldman earned diplomas in nursing and midwifery, then she returned to the United States to practice nursing and to renew her campaign to promote anarchy. She set out on a cross-country tour and attracted large audiences everywhere she went. She spoke on many subjects, ranging from anarchism to marriage to "Jews in America" and "The Effect of War on Workers." One comrade reported: "Every fiber of her being is electrified by the spirit to which her lips give utterance." She attracted admirers, gained converts, and incurred the wrath of those who said she was working for the devil. Over and over again, she was arrested and forced to spend nights in local jails.

Goldman eventually separated from Brady and accepted an offer from friends to pay her way through medical school in Switzerland. But while in England she met (and later fell in love with) Czechoslovakian anarchist Hippolyte Havel. Together, they took part in an underground meeting of the International Anarchist Congress. This led her friends in the U.S. who had agreed to support her in medical school to complain she was studying anarchy, not medicine. She responded that she no longer wanted their money. She would not allow anyone to tell her what to do. She and Havel left for New York, where they learned that Berkman had tried unsuccessfully to escape from prison and was frequently sent to solitary confinement. Goldman visited Berkman in prison and found him to be battered, thin, almost blind, and unable to speak. It was the first time she had seen him in nine years.

He had been severely crippled by his imprisonment and still had many years left to serve. This level of suffering led her to question if the cause was worth it. If it were, maybe they should use different techniques to accomplish their goals. She eventually decided that breaking laws for the cause was not productive and only harmed the movement. She ceased to believe the end justified the means. Anarchists must do more than destroy what held them in bondage; they must also strive to build a free society.

Her resolution was not shaken when Leon Czolgosz, an avowed anarchist, assassinated President William McKinley in September 1901. Headlines announced that Czolgosz admitted to the murder and claimed to be a follower of Emma Goldman. This incited a sometimes violent anti-anarchist campaign that spread through the country. In some cities anarchists were beaten and driven out of their homes; in others they were jailed for no reason except that they were openly anarchists.

"Red Emma" turned herself in to the Chicago police. She was charged with conspiracy. While awaiting trial

This painting depicts the assassination of President McKinley by Leon Czolgosz, a follower of Goldman. *(Library of Congress)*

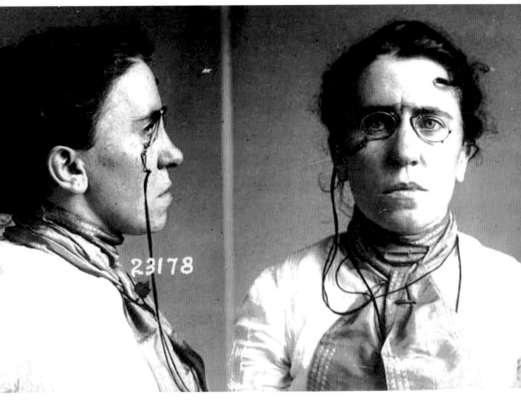

This mug shot of Goldman was taken after her 1901 arrest, based on charges of conspiracy to assassinate the president. *(Library of Congress)*

she was abused. At her trial she took the stand for herself, dressed demurely in a white blouse, navy skirt, and a straw hat with a veil. She calmly answered all questions put to her.

There was no evidence against her and the case was finally dropped. Goldman then tried unsuccessfully to rally support for Colgosz's defense. She was deeply disappointed that other anarchists would not come to his aid. From that time on, she had little to do with others in the anarchist movement. Goldman was thoroughly discouraged and felt only contempt for the cowardice of her fellow anarchists. She even changed her name. No longer "Red Emma," she was Miss Smith, a private nurse in the tenements on the East Side.

When she read of a new wave of persecutions in Russia, Goldman regained her eagerness to fight for her ideals. As she entered into her cause again, she criticized herself: "I am like the incurable drunkard. I have the best intentions to be reformed, to get away from people . . . [but] I fear I am forever doomed to remain public property."

The tide against anarchists remained strong in the United States. Theodore Roosevelt, the new president, warned against it. States passed laws making it a crime to advocate anarchy, and the U.S. Congress passed the Anarchist Exclusion Act, barring anarchists from entering the country.

But the twentieth century ushered a new spirit. Innovations such as the spread of electricity gave new vitality to Americans both commercially and privately. Greenwich Village became a place where innovative ideas such as suffrage for women and pacifism were discussed openly—creating greater acceptance for many of Goldman's views.

With financing in part from Russian immigrant and actor Paul Orleneff, Goldman launched a magazine on March 6, 1906, called *Mother Earth*. Edited by Goldman, the magazine was filled with articles on patriotism, love, anarchism, and women's liberation. The periodical was considered "a pioneer spokesman for radical thought in the twentieth century" with an emphasis on economic and labor issues. *Mother Earth* attracted not only anarchists, but also professional, middle-class readers.

Fourteen years after he had left for Pennsylvania, Berkman was released from prison. He returned to Goldman in New York, a broken man, both physically and emotionally. He was unresponsive for months, but when Goldman was arrested for criminal anarchy, he sprung back to life. "The struggle is going on, and I feel a great joy in my heart," he wrote. When she was freed, Goldman was able to leave Berkman in charge of *Mother Earth* while she made a cross-country speaking tour and attended the International Anarchist Congress in Amsterdam.

As she planned her trip home from Amsterdam, Goldman wondered if the Anarchist Exclusion Act would prevent her from returning to New York. It should not,

In 1906, Goldman began publishing *Mother Earth*, a magazine that dealt with anarchy, women's rights, and other social issues.

she reasoned, because it applied to aliens, not citizens, and she was a citizen. Still, she did not trust the United States government. She managed to escape from the government spies tracking her in London and sailed to Montreal, slipping into New York by train.

Goldman had underestimated the hostility of the U.S. government toward her. Immigration officials cited a technicality to show that her first husband, Kersner, was not a citizen, therefore voiding her claim to citizenship.

In Chicago, she was watched constantly by police and warned that she would not be allowed to make a speech. Public opinion was running strongly against anarchy. A San Diego editorial said "Hanging is none too good for them [anarchists]. They would be much better dead, for they are absolutely useless in the human economy. They are the waste material of creation and should be drained off into the sewer of oblivion there to rot in cold obstruction like any other excrement."

Goldman was ready to fight. She said a "powerful country [was] moving heaven and earth to gag one little woman. I will stay." Ben Reitman, the so-called Hobo King who had led a demonstration of the unemployed, helped her to set up a talk in the local Workmen's Hall, but police pulled Goldman out of the hall. On another night, after a speech, Reitman was herded into a car by vigilantes, beaten, and tortured.

Despite the majority attitude against anarchy, there were some that supported Goldman's right to free speech. There was a gradual move toward more freedom building in the country. Worldwide there were revolutions erupting in Russia, China, and Mexico, and intellectual ferment and assault on orthodoxy was developing all over the world.

At the same time, labor unions became more militant as strikers demanded better working conditions. Large strikes in Lawrence, Massachusetts. and Paterson, New Jersey, brought hundreds of supporters and activists together. Their supporters appealed to Congress, raised funds for strikers, and attended public demonstrations. The women's suffrage movement had won the vote in four states by 1910 and pushed forward to ratification of the nineteenth amendment in 1920.

All these movements energized Goldman. As she reached middle age, her glasses had thick lenses that magnified her eyes, and she paid little attention to her hair. Her smoking and drinking and her outspoken attitude toward sex and marriage shocked most people. Goldman saw this as a double standard of morality: men were allowed to have such freedom, but women were not.

Many citizens saw Goldman as a symbol of sin. Even the suffragists spoke against her. They believed that once women had the right to vote, they would be equal. Goldman believed that a complete change of society's attitude was needed before women could be equal. When she belittled the value of the vote, she turned people against her, as she did when she mocked religion, attacked patriotism in soldiers, smoked in public, and made no secret of practicing free love.

Goldman traveled throughout North America giving lectures, and her audiences steadily increased. In Winnipeg, Canada, she spoke to crowds of 1,500 and in San Francisco, 2,000. Between 1908 and 1917, she spoke three to five times a week. Police sometimes showed up to declare that a hall was unsafe, to stand outside to intimidate anyone who might want to attend, or to arrest Goldman for incitement to violence.

When Goldman supported the growing birth-control movement, she took on an even greater risk of arrest. At an open meeting in March 1915, she explained the methods of birth control and displayed birth control devices to a mixed audience of about six hundred people. This was a blatant disregard of a law forbidding such a talk and she was arrested early in 1916.

At her trial, Goldman said, "If it is a crime to work for healthy motherhood and happy child-life, I am proud to be considered a criminal." She was found guilty and sentenced to pay a $100.00 fine or to serve fifteen days in jail. She chose jail. As soon as she was released, she went back to her talks. She was arrested again and again, sometimes acquitted, sometimes sentenced to a short jail term.

By 1916, the United States still had not decided to join World War I, which had begun in 1914. Bitter conflict grew in the United States between those who supported American intervention and those who opposed it. Goldman believed that war was nothing but a tool of government. Then, as an audience of 100,000 watched a Preparedness Parade of citizens supporting intervention, someone detonated a bomb. Ten people were killed, and forty wounded. Newspapers declared the explosion to be the work of "anarchist bombs." Goldman was accused of the bombing, tried, and found innocent.

In 1917, President Woodrow Wilson asked the U.S. Congress to declare war on Germany. The United States erupted in a frenzy of anti-German feelings that swept up even many former pacifists. Wilson also signed a draft bill under which most young American men were subject to conscription.

In June 1917, forty-eight-year-old Goldman was tried with Berkman for speaking against the draft. It took the jury twenty-nine minutes to find them guilty. The judge imposed a sentence of two years in prison and a $10,000 fine for each defendant. He also recommended they be deported when their sentences were fulfilled. "For such people as would nullify our laws, we have no place in our country." Awaiting trial and while on appeal, Goldman was bailed out, but Berkman was held on a murder charge for another incident. Goldman arranged a mass rally for Berkman in a New York theater. A policeman threatened to arrest her if she spoke, so near the end of the meeting she appeared on the stage with a gag in her mouth. Later, the murder charges against Berkman were dropped.

The U.S. Supreme Court decided that Goldman and Berkman were guilty of conspiracy. Goldman told supporters: "Be of good cheer, good friends and comrades. We are going to prison with light hearts. To us it is more satisfactory to stay behind bars than to remain muzzled in freedom."

Goldman celebrated her fiftieth birthday in the Missouri State Prison. She declared, "if every rebel were sent to prison for a time, it would fan his smoldering flame of hate of the things that make prisons possible." She received streams of birthday cards and presents, all celebrating her courage and endurance. She insisted, "No one need worry about me. I am quite alright. I have my one Great Love—my Ideal, to sustain me, nothing else matters."

In prison she lived in a seven-by-eight-foot cell with one straw bag for a mattress and one for a pillow. She worked nine-hour shifts six days a week, making clothes for public sale. In her free time, she read about the growing revolution in Russia and dreamed of going there to help.

In September 1919, Goldman was released from prison. A month later she was summoned to Ellis Island for a deportation hearing. She was identified as a noncitizen on grounds that her marriage to Kersner had not been sufficient to grant her citizenship status. She was also charged with incitement to violence, publication of violent articles, and even a role in McKinley's assassination.

She briefly considered marriage to a United States citizen—two men in particular offered to be her husband—to avert deportation, but her lawyer told her it would not help.

At her deportation hearing Goldman refused to answer any questions. She did give a written statement: "I protest against these proceedings." Both Berkman and Goldman were freed until their cases were decided on appeal.

Eventually, a federal judge declared that Goldman was not a United States citizen and therefore would be deported. Berkman, who had never claimed to be a citizen, would also be deported. At first, Goldman savored each moment of returning to Russia, where she expected to find the "promise and hope of the world."

Early in the morning of December 21, 1919, Berkman, Goldman, and other deportees were taken to the barge the S.S. *Buiford,* where they were escorted by 250 guards carrying revolvers. Thirty-three years earlier Goldman had sailed into New York Harbor, disturbed by her memories of Russian soldiers beating prisoners. Now she left the same harbor with memories of United States police and soldiers abusing citizens.

Only a few days in Russia were enough to reveal to Goldman that the ideals of the Russian Revolution had not been fulfilled. People were hungry and poorly clothed, just as they had been under the czar. All criticism of the Bolsheviks, the rulers of the new Communist government, was shouted down as illegal counter-revolutionary speech. Bolshevik leaders insisted Russia could not yet afford the luxury of freedom. Goldman countered that no revolution should support so much injustice and brutality.

On December 21, 1921, Goldman and Berkman left for Latvia. Goldman said, "I must raise my voice against the crimes committed in the name of the Revolution." They looked for a home but no country would accept them. They fled from

Latvia to Sweden to Germany, a country that would accept them only on a month-by-month basis. In 1924, Berkman was able to settle in Germany, and Goldman made her home in England. There, Goldman wrote *My Disillusionment in Russia,* in which she accepted the premise that violence is necessary to create a revolution, but rejected violence as a way of life.

Goldman agreed to marry Jim Colton, a Welsh anarchist, in order to get a British passport and the privileges of a British citizen. Soon after the marriage she traveled to Canada for a yearlong lecture tour. There she was a popular speaker on anarchism, birth control, and literature.

In 1928, she retired to St. Tropez in the Mediterranean Sea to write her autobiography. Berkman left Germany to work near her. Three years later, sixty-three-year-old Goldman left St. Tropez with her two-volume autobiography *Living My Life.*

The next year the Great Depression hit every country in Europe as well as the United States, and a period of unemployment left millions without food, clothing, shelter, or hope. Some of the affected people became radicals, eager to turn power over to dictators such as Benito Mussolini and his Fascist Party in Italy, and Adolph Hitler and his Nazi Party in Germany. These men promised revolution and gave voice to the resentments of millions. They also built up strong feelings of national pride and proclaimed the patriots of his country to be a superior race. Both men used terror to come to power and to maintain it and made open threats against the other countries in Europe, Africa, and Asia. Goldman began to speak out against fascism and Nazism.

In 1935, a depressed and almost penniless Goldman returned to France, one of the few countries where Berkman was allowed to live. Goldman told him, "Men have come and gone in my long life. But you my dearest, will remain forever." Berkman replied that their life together was "one of the most beautiful and rarest things in the world." Then, on June 28, 1936, Goldman's sixty-seventh birthday, Berkman died from a self-inflicted gunshot wound—his answer to chronic pain and unrelenting poverty.

After Berkman's death, Goldman fell into a depression that lasted months. Then she was summoned to Spain to help Spanish anarchists resist the fascist takeover led by General Francisco Franco. Working people armed themselves against Franco and for a period of time it seemed that the anarchists were leading a successful revolution. Goldman directed the press and propaganda in England, a country whose support Goldman thought was necessary. Then anarchists in Spain decided to side with a government-supported movement, the Popular Front, and the situation deteriorated. In January 1939, General Franco took over the country.

On May 14, 1940, seventy-year-old Emma Goldman died of complications from a stroke. In death, she was finally allowed to return to the United States and was buried near the graves of other anarchists in Waldheim Cemetery in Chicago.

Emma Goldman lived her life as an outsider—as an anarchist and an exile. Her personal and professional life revealed a dual personality. Professionally, she wanted to be a role model for potential anarchists. Personally, she raised questions about the motivations in her life, once writing to a family member, "Did it not occur to you that my external activities may have been an escape from my emotional dissatisfaction deeply hidden in my inner life?"

Goldman was more a dynamic personality than an effective leader. She refused to compromise and was intolerant of criticism and did not often work effectively with union leaders, socialists, women's groups, or others. She chose to "bow to nothing except my idea of right." This was both her strength and her weakness.

Emma Goldman herself summed up her own life in her autobiography: "My life—I had lived in its heights and its depths, in bitter sorrow and ecstatic joy, in black despair and fervent hope. I had drunk the cup to the last drop. I had lived my life . . . in many of my more important actions and attitudes, I would repeat my life as I have lived it."

EMMA GOLDMAN
—•— timeline —•—

1869 Born June 27 in Kovno, Russia.

1885 Immigrates to the United States with sister, Helena.

1886 Finds work in a factory as a garment worker; riot breaks out in Haymarket Square in Chicago after workers demonstrate for eight-hour day.

1887 Marries fellow worker Jacob A. Kersner; becomes enraged at the injustice of the execution of four anarchists connected to the Haymarket bombing.

1888 Divorces Kersner; moves briefly to New Haven.

1889 Arrives in New York with a sewing machine and five dollars; meet Alexander (Sasha) Berkman and Johann Most.

1892 Reacts to news of shooting deaths of nine steel workers during strike at Carnegie Steel Company; plots with Berkman to assassinate the plant manager of Carnegie Steel; Berkman found guilty and sentenced to twenty-two years in prison; meets Austrian anarchist Edward Brady.

1893 Sentenced to one year in prison for inciting violence.

1894 Released from prison; supports herself working as a nurse; moves in with Brady.

1895 Leaves United States for Europe; earns diplomas in nursing and midwifery before returning to U.S.

1901 Implicated in the assassination of U.S. president William McKinley; turns herself in to Chicago police; case dropped.

1906 Launches magazine called *Mother Earth*; Berkman released from prison.

1917 The United States enters World War II; tried, found guilty, and jailed for speaking against draft.

1919 Released from prison; deported from United States, along with Berkman, to Russia.

1925 Marries Jim Colton, a Welsh anarchist.

1928 Retires to St. Tropez in Mediterranean Sea to write autobiography.

1935 Berkman dies; falls into depression.

1940 Dies of complications from stroke; buried in Chicago near Haymarket anarchists.

Upton Sinclair
(Library of Congress)

three
Upton Sinclair:

"My Cause is the Cause of a man who has never yet been defeated, and whose whole-being is one all devouring God-given holy purpose"

Bedbugs—those reddish-brown smelly beetles no bigger than a pencil eraser—helped Upton Sinclair to win a Pulitzer Prize. When he was a boy he had to deal with bedbugs. At night, as soon as the bedroom lights were out, the bugs came scurrying into his bed, searching for human blood. Young Upton, sleeping at the foot of his parents' bed, would feel first one, then two, then a half a dozen or more bites. He would slap at them and yell until his mother would switch on the light. Suddenly there would be no bugs to be seen. Through years of evolution, bedbugs had come to fear light and disappear almost as fast as the human eye could spot them.

For Upton, the bugs created an itch that was more than skin-deep, an itch that could not be scratched away. It was a deep feeling that no person should have to live in a situation where he could not sleep at night. The young boy knew that not everyone had to sleep with bedbugs. There

Bedbugs are nocturnal insects that feed on the warm blood of humans and other mammals.

were no bedbugs in the luxurious home where he visited his wealthy Aunt Priscilla and Uncle Bland.

Upton's father, Upton Beall Sinclair, was an alcoholic. When his father was out drinking, Upton was sometimes sent out to search the bars and help to bring his staggering father home. Walking his father home was better than returning and telling his mother he could not find him. Then, he and his mother, once a member of the Southern aristocracy, could only wait and worry.

Upton, born on September 20, 1878, taught himself to read when he was about five years old. A doctor declared he was too fragile to go to school so he stayed at home and taught himself until he entered public school at age ten. He passed through eight elementary grades in two years. Books were his company, and he loved them more than anything else. He used them to escape from the boardinghouse room or insults that came from his snobby aunt. Books took him to desert islands or other countries.

When Upton was ten years old, in 1888, he and his mother moved to New York City to be close to his maternal grandparents. Whenever his mother decided the poverty was too hard on her son, she sent him either to his grandparents or to his aunt and uncle. Later Upton wrote: "My life was a series of Cinderella transformations; one night I would be sleeping on a vermin-ridden sofa in a lodging house, and the next night under silken coverlets in a fashionable home." He often asked his mother why some people were so poor and some so rich. She did not have an answer.

Upton's mother insisted they attend a fashionable Episcopal church. Upton's resentment of the wealthy grew at church. He and his mother had to sit in the back pews because they could not afford to tithe to the church. Regardless, she bought the best clothes she could afford to wear to church. He remembered: "always I wore tight new shoes and tight gloves and a neatly brushed little derby hat—supreme discomfort to the glory of God."

"I was an extraordinarily devout little boy; one of my earliest recollections—I cannot have been more than four years of age—is of carrying a dust-broom about the house as a choir-boy carried the golden cross every Sunday morning," he later remembered. He considered Jesus to be one of his heroes.

But when he began teaching Sunday school around age fifteen, Upton began to doubt religion. Did God really rescue Jonah from the whale and Moses from the bulrushes? If He did all this rescuing, why didn't He rescue Upton's father from drinking. Why didn't He rescue Upton from the bedbugs? Why didn't He feed the starving baby next door?

When a friend of Upton's was arrested, he told Upton a story when he was released. He said a minister had visited him in jail, prayed with him, and left. Then a leader from

Tammany Hall, the Democratic Party organization, visited the boy and had seen to it he was set free. Upton decided the church was all talk and that politics was action.

Because he moved often, Upton learned to fit into different social situations. In some locations, he entertained himself with books. In New York City, he roamed with gangs, swiped food from greengrocers, and harassed drivers of horse-drawn wagons and automobiles by dodging through streets on roller skates.

As a teenager, Upton admired the work and life of Romantic English poet and essayist Percy Bysshe Shelley. In a book about the philosophy of reform, Shelley wrote of European governments in which a few selfish leaders have used the fears of the ignorant to establish their own power and to destroy the hope and interest of the many. As Upton read, his resentment of the social class system became a revolutionary fervor. He resolved he would lead people to demand a classless society.

As a child often left to himself, Upton had explored his abilities to see, hear, smell, touch, and taste, and had developed a habit of recording his experiences, both in notes and in mental recollections. These habits—plus his wide reading experiences—created a talent for storytelling. Without being conscious of it, he had been practicing the writer's craft.

Upton began writing stories for money after he enrolled at the College of the City of New York, in 1892, just after his fourteenth birthday. The first story he sold was about an innocent young black man accused of arson. This story was published in a magazine called *Argosy*, and he was paid $25. He branched out into joke-writing, which became a steady source of money. He worked on his jokes all the time:

"I kept my little notebook before me at meals, while walking, while dressing, and in college if the professor was a bore." One example of an Upton Sinclair joke, for which he was paid $1.00: "*Old Lady*: You look as if you never washed, sir. *Weary Will*: Yes, Ma'am; I prefer godliness."

His writing paid his way through Columbia University, where he studied philosophy and literature with thoughts of a career in law. He continued to write fast. "I kept two secretaries working all the time, taking dictation one day and transcribing the next." He published voluminously in magazines while studying full-time at Columbia, plus a series of nickel novels written under the pen names Lieutenant Frederick Garrison and Ensign Clarke Fitch.

As graduation time approached, his Uncle Bland offered to train him for a bank job, but Sinclair refused. He would not work for any business that catered to the wealthy.

He became more and more hostile toward his family and the world around him—toward his father because of his drunkenness, and toward his mother for not trying to relieve the family's poverty, toward churches for their hypocrisy, and toward all wealthy people. He resolved to write a novel that would incorporate all these problems. He worked on it for several months, but it did not come easily: "The burden of my spirit had become greater than I could carry. The vision of life that had come to me must be made known to the rest of the world."

While working on the novel, he continued writing articles for money. In one article, titled "Offertory," Sinclair discussed how he had changed from a reverent awe-inspired, teenage Sunday school teacher into an adult who saw that the trappings of the church "were nothing but a bait, a device to lure the poor into the trap of submission to their exploiters."

During this time he met eighteen-year-old Meta Fuller, a young woman who liked to listen to him talk about his goals. Sinclair told her: "You were given to me to master and make of you what you ought to be." She answered, "I bow in joy before you." They married in 1900.

Sinclair wrote *Springtime and Harvest,* which he was convinced was the "Great American Novel." It is a story of a beautiful woman who marries a crippled man for his money. No publisher would accept the manuscript, so Sinclair published it himself. Not counting copies he gave to his friends, he sold only two books. While he and Meta awaited the birth of their first child, Sinclair wrote *Prince Hagen* about a dwarf who arrives on Wall Street with a treasure of gold.

Meta and Sinclair's son David was born in December 1900. This addition to their family made their troubled financial situation even worse. In 1902, in a cost-cutting measure, the young family moved into a tent on a remote island in Lake Erie.

In financial desperation, Sinclair published *The Journal of Arthur Stirling,* claiming it was the autobiography of a poet who had just committed suicide. To reinforce the hoax, he inserted notices of the "death" of Arthur Stirling in New York papers. Although the book got some favorable reviews for its emotion and drama, sales failed to meet his financial needs.

Four of Sinclair's novels were published between 1901 and 1906, but none sold well. Each was considered a typical, undistinguished Romantic novel like so many others published in that time. Financially desperate and deeply discouraged, he stopped working on his writing and moved back with his mother and father, leaving his wife and son.

Disenchanted with his writing, Sinclair turned his interest towards politics. He was drawn to socialism, a political system in which government controlled most of the means of production and managed all the essential needs, such as transportation, electricity, education, and health resources. Attending Socialist Party meetings gave him new purpose: "I did not have to carry the whole burden of humanity's future upon my two frail shoulders," he realized. He wasn't concerned that socialism was unpopular and looked down upon by most Americans.

Sinclair also did not seem to be concerned that Meta did not have enough money for food, even though their son David needed a special diet that was expensive and their roof leaked. He did not even seem to care when Meta looked elsewhere for companionship.

When Sinclair received an advance from a publisher for a trilogy of Civil War books, he moved his tent to some woods near Princeton, New Jersey, to have access to excellent Civil War papers at the nearby university library.

After he had finished only the first volume of the trilogy, Sinclair received a new assignment, and a $400 cash advance, to write the work that would become the most sensational book in his career. The publisher of America's most read Socialist newspaper, *The Appeal to Reason*, wanted him to document the lives of the stockyard workers in Chicago.

The invention of the refrigerated railroad car in 1879 had made it possible to ship packaged meat great distances. Entrepreneurs partnered with owners of railroads to buy cattle in large quantities, build huge stockyards

Sinclair's successful novel, *The Jungle,* was based on the unsanitary and unsafe working conditions of meat processing factories. *(Library of Congress)*

and packing plants, and to butcher the meat and ship it all over the country.

In order to keep down costs at the stockyards the pay was low and the conditions were miserable. Any worker who complained about low wages or poor working conditions was quickly fired and replaced with one of the stream of immigrants flooding into America. There was little competition in the meatpacking industry, and owners could pay workers as little as they wanted to and could set prices as high as they wished.

Disguised as a worker in shabby clothes with a dinner pail, Sinclair went to Chicago and toured some of the stockyards and processing plants. The working conditions were unsanitary beyond belief, and the workers he met were so mired in debt to their employers that they were virtual slaves.

When he returned home from Chicago, after seven weeks of research, Sinclair spent little time with his wife and son. He holed up in an eight-by-ten-foot shack that had one window and a pot-bellied, coal burning stove. His itch to reform the world was stronger than ever and he hoped this new novel would shock readers and begin a strong movement toward socialism, which he was convinced was the only way to free the powerless workers.

In the manuscript, Sinclair spared potential readers no ugly details about what the workers' daily lives were like. He described the meat packing plants where workers routinely lost limbs and sometimes drowned in vats of oil. Sinclair decided he would title his new book *The Jungle,* and hoped it would repulse and outrage its readers.

Sinclair said that the story of *The Jungle*'s hero, Jurgis Rudkus, and his family was similar to the story of his own family. "Did I wish to know how the poor suffered in winter time in Chicago? I only had to recall the previous winter in the cabin, when we had only cotton blankets, and had rags on top of us. It was the same with hunger, with illness, with fear. Our little boy was down with pneumonia that winter and the grief of that went into the book."

Again and again in the novel, Jurgis falls back on his conviction that if he only works harder, everything will be all right. But the birth of a second child, his wife's complications from child birth, his own badly sprained ankle, and the theft

UPTON SINCLAIR 132-11

A young Upton Sinclair *(Library of Congress)*

of his money by a family member are all blows to his faith in hard work. After a series of misfortunes, Jurgis becomes a committed socialist and part of the socialist movement in Chicago.

Sinclair's novel was rejected by six publishers. A typical comment was this one from an editor at Macmillan: "I advise without hesitation and unreservedly against the publication of this book which is gloom and horror unrelieved. One feels that what is at the bottom of his [Sinclair's] fierceness is not nearly so much desire to help the poor as hatred of the rich."

He published and tried to market the book himself but sold fewer than one thousand copies. The publishing company Doubleday then decided to publish it—and *The Jungle* was an immediate success.

Later when he spoke about the immense popularity of *The Jungle*, Sinclair expressed disappointment that readers were deeply moved by the scenes in the stockyards but relatively unmoved by the books anti-capitalist message. "I aimed at the public's heart, and by accident I hit it in the stomach," he remarked.

His vision was of a socialist country, and his goal had been to reform, not to write a popular novel. He had hoped the book would make clear beyond question that the American society and economic system was a failure and that it did not live up to American ideals. When his main character turned socialist at the end of the book, Sinclair wanted readers to feel empathy for his life, not just sympathy.

The book did have a strong impact, though. It inspired a government investigation of the meat-packing industry and focused public sentiment on reforming the industry to make it safer for workers and consumers.

The novel also inspired contempt from some. President Theodore Roosevelt had coined the term "muckrakers" to label writers who, in his opinion, exceeded the bounds of common decency in their fervor to root out corruption. Many critics considered *The Jungle* to be a muckraking book that exaggerated conditions in the meatpacking houses to create sensationalism and to make money for the author and publisher.

Still, muckrakers were sometimes effective at undermining what had often been an almost unquestioning attitude about business practices in America on the part of the public. President Roosevelt said he disagreed with the book's socialist message, but he admitted that "radical action must be taken to do away with the efforts of arrogant and selfish greed on the part of the capitalist."

The meatpacker Armour and Company responded to *The Jungle* by saying, "not one atom of any condemned animal or carcass finds its way, directly or indirectly, from any source, into any food product or food ingredient." Sinclair answered with a list of specific charges against Armour and Company,

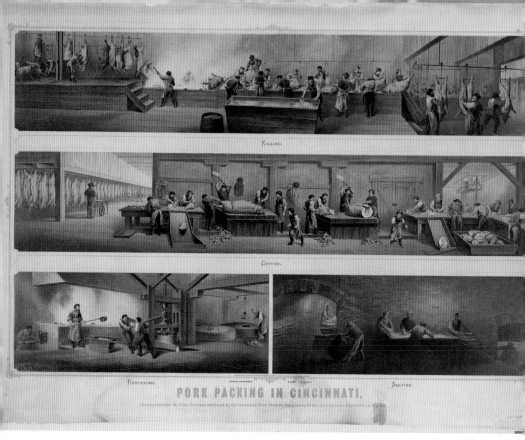

PORK PACKING IN CINCINNATI.

Photo depicting the operation of a slaughterhouse *(Library of Congress)*

openly inviting a libel suit by asking that the dispute be settled in a court of law.

Meanwhile, federal investigators presented President Roosevelt with a report that impelled him to ask the U.S. Congress to pass a law mandating federal inspection for meat intended for domestic consumption. This law, the Pure Food and Drug Act of 1906, also prohibited the sale of adulterated food products.

With royalties of about $30,000 from *The Jungle*, Sinclair established a socialist commune, the Helicon Home Colony in Englewood, New York. His plans called for hundreds of residents to eventually live at the commune, although it began with just twelve in its first winter, 1906. Sinclair said Helicon Home Colony was an effort at cooperative living, not a socialist colony. All residents would take part in the upkeep of the place, from tending the furnaces to cooking to caring for the children.

While he lived at Helicon, Sinclair wrote *The Industrial Republic*, prophesying the coming of socialism to America. But after only four months in operation, the commune burned to the ground. Suddenly, Sinclair was broke again, having tied most of his money up in the project. Later he blamed those who opposed his ideas for starting the fire, although no proof was found to back up his charge.

Sinclair hoped that the enthusiasm for *The Jungle* would transfer to sales for his new book, *The Metropolis*, a story that featured wealthy society characters. When his hopes did not materialize he blamed poor writing—not that his vision of socialism was not striking a receptive chord with the reading public. He blamed the poor writing on lack of time, a consequence of his lack of money. "Never have I been able to write a single thing as I would have liked it, because of money."

Sinclair fell into a depression. He continued to shock the public. He said publicly that marriage was "nothing but legalized slavery" and pointed out Meta's infidelity, though he did not mention his neglect of her. His great dream of a commune had gone up in smoke. His books were not selling well, and he received fewer contracts and smaller advances. He tried to improve his health and outlook with fasting and special diets, but nothing worked.

In *Samuel the Seeker*, his main character is a fictionalized version of himself. Samuel is cheated by his employers and by his clergymen. He becomes a Socialist and is beaten during a demonstration against capitalism.

In 1912, Sinclair and Meta divorced. Despite his earlier criticisms of marriage, he soon married Mary Craig Kimbrough, a friend of Meta's and an aristocratic Southern beauty. When later discussing her marriage to Sinclair, Mary said, "I feel that my life has been worthwhile because I have rescued Upton from melancholia and perhaps death. And I know he is a great and high factor in the betterment of mankind." She took charge of Sinclair's finances and managed his relationship with his son David, as well as his social contacts. She also critiqued his writing.

In 1914, miners in the Colorado Fuel and Iron Company went on strike. The managers of the company, which was owned by John D. Rockefeller, hired a group of private detectives that specialized in breaking ups strikes to force the workers back into the mine. The detectives shot at striking miners and set fire to their temporary homes. Twenty people were killed, though no one was arrested for the killings.

An angry Sinclair wrote to Rockefeller: "I intend this night to indict you upon a charge of murder. . . . But before I take this step, I wish to give you every opportunity of fair play."

Sinclair was arrested for taking part in a demonstration. When he refused to pay a $3.00 fine, he was jailed. From jail he wrote about how Rockefeller brutalized and murdered his workers, whom Sinclair called slaves. He went on a hunger strike to publicize his message, pointing to Mahatma Gandhi as his guide for nonviolent protests. Gandhi was a Hindu born in India in the late nineteenth century. First as a lawyer, then as a philosopher and teacher, Gandhi taught a philosophy of passive resistance to injustice. Gandhi was frequently jailed for leading protests, and during his incarcerations, he often fasted.

This photograph shows Sinclair (right) picketing the Rockefeller building. (*Library of Congress*)

Perhaps partly due to the intervention of Mary's socially prominent mother, Sinclair was released. Once freed, he refused to drop his fight against imprisonment for political views. He said "when I see a line of a hundred policemen with drawn revolvers flung across a street . . . I have a conscience and a religious faith, and I know that our liberties were not won without suffering, and may be lost again through cowardice."

Sinclair did not accept Gandhi's commitment to nonviolence, claiming that violence might be needed to preserve democracy. He said class conflict would continue to escalate as long as unions were not allowed to organize, rights to public assembly were denied, and public elections were fraudulently run by corporation officials who marked ballots for illiterate voters.

Partly because of his fame as a writer, Sinclair was asked to accept the Socialist Party nomination to be its candidate for the U.S. Congress from New Jersey. He accepted but did no campaigning because, as he said, he had more important things to do. Of the 24,000 votes cast, he received 750.

He continued to write novels advocating socialism. From 1907 to 1915, he wrote about a book a year, most of which were commercially unsuccessful. Critics said they were merely socialist propaganda thinly disguised as novels. His books were more popular in Japan, however.

War loomed in Europe. The causes of the conflict were numerous: nationalism, the desire for countries to expand its influence and to control parts of the world, an arms race, social turmoil brought on by rapid industrialization, and miscalculations by rulers and generals. In the United States, public opinion was against getting involved in the European conflict when World War I began in the summer of 1914.

As the European war continued, however, the United States was clearly being drawn into the conflict. Finally, in 1917, President Woodrow Wilson declared that United States involvement was needed and declared war on Germany and its allies.

Sinclair was initially opposed to American involvement in the war, but as the war wore on he changed his mind. He wrote to members of the Anti-Enlistment League, which was organized to advocate for neutrality, that he admired them, but "I believe in the present effort which the Allies are making to suppress German militarism. I would approve of America going to their assistance."

The Socialist Party opposed the war, so Sinclair dropped his party membership. He said that "if Germany be allowed to win this war—then we in America shall have to drop every other activity and devote the next twenty or thirty years to preparing for a last-ditch of the democratic principle."

He started a new magazine, *Upton Sinclair's,* to appeal to young Socialists, Nationalists, and other liberal groups to support the war. On the masthead was the motto: "A Clean Peace and the International." He dismissed without comment the many refusals of would-be subscribers and the hate mail. He said, "I grant every man the right to disagree with me—the more the merrier, it is all advertising." The magazine folded in just a few months.

Propaganda came from both sides. Those supporting Germany and the Central Powers insisted that the Allies had caused the war and that Germany was fighting to save western Europe from French and Russian aggression. Those supporting America and the Allies insisted that the Germans, especially with their experiments with new weapons like submarines and poison gas, were determined to conquer the world and to demand total obedience to authority with no individual freedom. The war ended in 1919, when German Kaiser Wilhelm II stepped down.

Sinclair did not stop writing during the war. He had moved to California and from there wrote thirty plays, most on the need for reform. In 1919, he wrote the play *Cicero: A Tragic Drama in Three Acts,* in which he attempted to show the similarities between problems of ancient Rome and those of the United States. After many rehearsals the play was performed in a small theater in New York City, but it flopped. He also wrote *The Profits of Religion,* in which he declared that institutionalized religion was based on exploitation of human fears and opposed all progressive changes in society.

For the next several years, Sinclair spent most of his time writing. In his work, he continued his attack on organized religion. He also began to criticize journalism and the failure of mass media to deal with the significant issues of the day and its attraction to sensationalism. In *The Goose Step*, he charged that higher education was controlled by the same kind of men who run major businesses and for the same goal of making money. He accused the faculty and administration of conspiring to indoctrinate students to have an unquestioning acceptance of capitalism. He followed this book with *The Goslings,* in which he charged that the corruption and fraud in lower-level education were as dangerous as those in higher education.

In 1923, he began writing a weekly column for the popular *New York American.* He used the column to criticize capitalism and to speak out for civil rights. When transport workers went on strike in California and were treated brutally by police, Sinclair traveled to speak to the crowds in support of the strikers and was arrested.

With the help of a colleague, he discovered that the police were planning to deny him bail. When he threatened to expose this unconstitutional act the police backed down. Sinclair was helped in this fight by the American Civil Liberties Union (ACLU), an organization founded in 1920 to guard the nation's constitutional liberties.

Meanwhile, although busy with his writing and other activities, Sinclair ran on the Socialist ticket for U.S. Congress in 1920 and for the U.S. Senate in 1922. He was unsuccessful in both races. He rejoined the Socialist Party as its candidate for governor of California in 1926. His platform, which included pardons for more than a thousand antiwar prisoners, turned many against him, as did an editorial in the *Los Angeles Times* labeling him as a proponent of free love. Despite the bad publicity, he received 900,000 votes.

In 1927, in a political novel titled *Boston,* he delved into the worldwide debate over the famous Sacco and Vanzetti case. Nicola Sacco and Bartolomeo Vanzetti were Italian

Nicola Sacco and Bartolomeo Vanzetti

immigrants who were arrested for robbery and murder in Massachusetts. The evidence against them was sketchy, but after a six-week trial they were found guilty of murder and sentenced to death. The sentence created an outcry among American liberals, Socialists (including Sinclair), and Communists, all of whom believed the men had not been given fair treatment. Although the case received worldwide attention and most people outside of the United States were convinced there was no adequate evidence for their conviction, they were electrocuted. On August 23, 1977, fifty years to the day of the executions of Sacco and Vanzetti, Michael S. Dukakis, then governor of Massachusetts, issued a proclamation stating that "Any stigma and disgrace shall be forever removed from their names."

Sinclair completed a book almost every year. Although none sold well, he managed to remain well known. He received dozens of letters a day, requests from all over the world for help, crank letters, and a pile of manuscripts by aspiring writers who wanted his comments. Sinclair answered every one of the aspiring writers.

He became fascinated with telepathic power, the ability to see what is invisible to others. Mary claimed to have telepathic powers, and together they studied psychic research and performed experiments. In one experiment, Sinclair gave Mary a drawing sealed in an envelope. Without touching the envelope, she attempted to make a copy of the drawing. Sinclair reported that "The results were amazing to us both." He provided details of these tests and more than two hundred others in a book titled *Mental Radio*.

The main character of Sinclair's 1937 novel *The Flivver King* was automobile tycoon and staunch anti-unionist Henry

Ford. A union leader later remembered, "There was a time when you could not walk into a union hall in Michigan without seeing the green covers of *The Flivver King* sticking out of the back pocket of a union man."

Already unpopular with conservatives and anti-Socialists, Sinclair became even more controversial when he encouraged Russian movie director Serge Mikhailovich to come to Hollywood, where Mary offered him a contract to produce a movie. Russia was controlled by the Communist Party under dictator Josef Stalin, whom many Americans saw as a grave threat. Mikhailovich was ordered back to Russia before he completed the project, and both Mary and Sinclair were left with debts from the failed project.

The Great Depression, beginning with the stock market crash in October 1929, and the massive unemployment it caused, gave a new impetus to the Socialist's movement in the United States. In 1930, when the Socialist Party again asked Sinclair to run for governor in California, he said he would if he did not have to spend time campaigning. "I know I can accomplish a hundred times as much for Socialism [by writing books] as I can by traveling about making speeches." Through letters and a few speeches, he proposed a platform that included teachers' rights to unionize and to receive adequate retirement salary, and enactment of state and inheritance taxes. He was defeated.

In 1934 he ran again for governor of California. This time he won considerable support for his End Poverty in California (EPIC) Program, which he argued was necessary because of rising unemployment. Although bread was only a nickel a loaf and steak eight cents a pound, many people did not have enough money to buy it. He wanted the government to

IMMEDIATE EPIC

The Final Statement of The Plan

By

UPTON SINCLAIR

The book, "I, Governor of California, And How I Ended Poverty," was written in August, 1933, and has been for a year the best selling book in the history of the State.

But meantime the crisis has deepened, and California draws every day nearer to bankruptcy.

Plans for bond issues, which seemed practicable a year ago, are seen in September of 1934 to involve too great delay.

The EPIC Plan has been revised in the light of a full year's criticism. We have learned from our friends how to improve the Plan, and from our enemies how to present it more effectively.

This is the final statement of the Plan, and supersedes all other statements.

PRICE 15 CENTS

END POVERTY LEAGUE
1501 SOUTH GRAND AVE.
LOS ANGELES, CALIFORNIA

The front cover of Sinclair's End Poverty in California (EPIC) plan (*Social Security Administration History Archives*) give people enough money to buy food. EPIC's opponents dubbed it Empty Promises in California. During the campaign, except for some statistics about this proposed program, Sinclair usually spoke without notes. He said he did not need reminding because his comments were about matters that had been deep in his heart for years. In the election he received almost 900,000 votes of the 2,300,000 cast. He summarized the election: "What beat us was money, then more money—and still more money."

The campaign left him deeply in debt. He worked to pay it off by lecturing and debating and by selling his books to the audiences after he spoke. In 1938, on his sixtieth birthday, he announced that he had just published his sixtieth book, *Little Steel: The Labor Movement in Fiction and Nonfiction.* He tried to earn money writing for the movies but was unsuccessful. His other writing fared better. *World's End,* an eleven-volume series on American government, in which his protagonist Lanny Budd encounters world-renowned figures such as Adolph Hitler and Franklin Roosevelt and becomes involved in international political intrigues, became a best-selling series.

Dragon's Teeth was the most successful of the series, and won the Pulitzer Prize. The book was an expression of Sinclair's philosophy and, as he had with *The Jungle,* he did not disguise his attempt to influence the reader. He based it on personal research and investigation of the situations pictured. His inclusion of material from his personal experiences made the work seem more real to readers. He said in his autobiography, *American Outpost,* "I wrote [*Dragon's Teeth*] with tears and anguish, pouring into the pages all the pain that life had meant to me."

Suffering from poor health, Mary gradually became reclusive. She refused to wear false teeth and leave the house, and Sinclair went to movies and dinner parties alone. He was also estranged from his son David.

Sinclair became convinced that he was being pursued by Communist assassins, and he and Mary moved frequently from one small California town to another. Finally, they settled in the small town of Monrovia where Sinclair spent most of his waking time writing, still trying to produce a book a year. Most critics continued to pan his work, calling it a rehash of his political campaigns and his political experiences and views.

In the 1950s, Mary supervised the collection and storage of Sinclair's books and papers. He wrote, "I had what was estimated to be over a quarter of a million letters.

. . . I had practically all the original manuscripts of my eighty books, and also of the pamphlets and circulars." These were housed in the library at Indiana University.

By 1954, a series of heart attacks had incapacitated Mary, and Sinclair spent most of his time caring for her. She died on April 26, 1961.

Less than six months after Mary's death, eighty-three-year-old Sinclair married Mary Elizabeth Willis, a seventy-nine-year-old widow. Sinclair said, "I'm sure I'm marrying one of the finest women in the world." They lived together, apparently happily, until she died six years later.

On November 25, 1968, Upton Beall Sinclair died in his sleep at an Arizona nursing home. He had summed up his life in his autobiography, *The Autobiography of Upton Sinclair.* In it Sinclair listed some of his accomplishments:

> 1. ended "slavery" of many workers

2. warned business owners against unfair employment practices
3. added to research in psychic phenomena
4. helped organize American Civil Liberties Union
5. changed the tone of California politics with his EPIC program
6. spread the socialistic movement into universities
7. contributed to the development of democratic ideas in Japan where his books were widely read
8. won the Pulitzer Prize for his Lanny Budd books

As a child, Sinclair had asked why some people had bedbugs and others had satin sheets in their bedrooms. He continued asking this question throughout his life. "I believe what I have believed ever since I discovered the socialist movement at the beginning of this century."

UPTON SINCLAIR

—•— timeline —•—

1878 Born September 20, 1878.

1892 Enrolls in the City College of New York; first
story published in a magazine.

1900 Marries Meta Fuller; son, David, born.

1901 Self-publishes *Springtime and Harvest;* sells
two copies.

1906 Gains fame with sixth novel, *The Jungle*; uses royalties
to establish a commune in New York state; runs as
a Socialist Party candidate for Congress and loses;
writes *The Industrial Republic.*

1907 Fire destroys commune.

1908 *Metropolis* published.

1912 Ends marriage to Meta Fuller.

1913 Marries second wife, Mary Craig Kimbrough.

1914 Jailed for two days for taking part in a demonstration
against the killing of twenty striking miners in
Colorado.

1918 Launches a new magazine, *Upton Sinclair's*; writes *The Profits of Religion*.

1919 Writes *Cicero: A Tragic Drama in Three Acts*.

1920 Runs for Congress on the Socialist ticket and loses.

1922 Loses race for U.S. Senate.

1923 Begins writing a weekly column for *New York American*.

1926 Loses race for governor of California.

1927 Novel *Boston* released.

1930 Loses second bid for governor's seat in California.

1934 Runs as Democratic candidate for governor of California; loses race.

1938 Publishes his sixtieth book at age sixty.

1943 Wins Pulitzer Prize for *Dragon's Teeth*.

1954 Second wife, Mary Craig Kimbrough, dies; marries third wife, Mary Elizabeth Willis.

1968 Dies in sleep at Arizona Nursing Home.

Norman Thomas
(Courtesy of Corbis)

four

Norman Thomas:

"Social justice makes better men"

When Norman Mattoon Thomas was growing up in Marion, Ohio, the other boys called him a sissy. He always dropped out before he finished a race and sometimes suffered from attacks of croup so bad they made him cough and choke as if he were suffocating. It wasn't just the other boys who made his life difficult—his teachers complained about him too. He was born left-handed on November 20, 1884, and at that time, many believed it was wrong to be left-handed. Teachers insisted that he use his right hand for writing, even though his left hand held the pencil more securely.

Whenever Norman could, he ran away from children who made fun of him and from the adults who criticized him. Safely alone, he immersed himself in books and reading. He loved stories about heroes who fought many obstacles in order to do the right thing. When he had read and reread everything for his level, he would pick up his father's books about theology and try to understand them.

He went to Sunday school twice a week. His father, Welling Thomas, was minister of the Presbyterian Church in Marion, Ohio, and enforced the strict rules of his religion. There was no card playing—or even playing marbles for keeps—dancing, or going to the theater. Norman's mother's name was Emma Mattoon Thomas, and he never forgot her story of how she had endured taunts as the daughter of a "Yankee carpetbagger" who taught blacks in a Presbyterian college in North Carolina.

Norman's parents did not coddle him. Besides going to school and doing homework, he milked the cow, stacked wood, washed dishes, and once a year he helped his mother with her spring cleaning—washing, hauling, folding, moving, and rug beating. Norman earned money soliciting subscriptions for church papers, distributing books to members of a book club, and picking berries for a penny a quart.

As he grew up, his health improved and he was able to take part in school life. Norman still loved reading, however, and kept trying to understand his father's theological books. Maybe it was these books, together with his father's sermons, that gave Norman a vision of making the world a better place. He borrowed books by Sir Walter Scott, Charles Dickens, Edward Gibbon's *Decline and Fall of the Roman Empire*, and other history books from the public library. His reading prepared him for the debating club, where he excelled.

Norman staged the first of many protests in his senior year. He was president of his class, and the school superintendent announced that, as usual, each senior would give a speech at graduation. Norman persuaded his classmates to

With his uncle's help, Thomas attended Princeton University. *(Library of Congress)*

protest that they wanted an outside speaker. In an effort to stop protests, the superintendent said the group could not meet on school grounds. Norman recalled later, "We stuck together, appointed committees, met off the school grounds, and campaigned for support from our parents, the town and members of the school board." Eventually, the students won, and a lawyer spoke at their graduation.

After graduation, Norman went to Bucknell University, a Baptist school, but did not feel challenged there. He eagerly accepted his uncle's offer to help him go to Princeton, where, after the first term, he was an A student. He cheered for Princeton's athletic teams, sang in the glee club, played flute in the orchestra, and served on the varsity debating team. He had to earn money on his time off. One summer he worked at a chair factory; another summer he sold aluminum cookware door-to-door.

Norman graduated in 1905, Phi Beta Kappa, and valedictorian of his class. After graduation he took a job with the neighborhood center of a Presbyterian church on Manhattan's lower West Side and was plunged into the problems of big city poverty, ignorance, and degradation—all new to him. He saw reeking tenements, open sewers, and people barely getting by despite working long hours at backbreaking jobs. He later wrote of one typical scene, in which he found himself sitting "on a broken chair, watching roaches and vermin making irregular patterns on grimy, broken plaster walls, comforting a sick woman on a filthy bed around which dirty toddlers played."

One of his responsibilities with the center was to intervene in gang wars. He quickly learned that no one person could do anything to stop gang violence. An intervention of many people, as well as money and other resources, were needed to deal with the problem.

At one point a child asked Thomas to help because her father, a drunken longshoreman, was threatening to kill his sick wife with an axe. Thomas managed to persuade the man to put away the axe but realized the axe could very well be brought out the next day. He asked himself what he could do to keep that axe—and all the other physical and emotional tools of cruelty—away from innocent sufferers. What could he do to try to stop the cycle of poverty, unemployment, unattended illness, and unrelieved desperation?

Thomas was certain that "social justice makes better men." He wrote that "Poverty was very great, strong liquor the chief escape, and much of the neighborhood was lost in a kind of sodden apathy." The job made him ever more aware of the gap between the "Haves and Have-Nots."

Thomas was not alone in coming to see how devastating the disparity in wealth and opportunity was. During the last years of the nineteenth century and first decades of the twentieth, large industrial unions were taking shape and a

In this photo, a poor child in New York City eats a meal on the street. Thomas believed that a public acceptance of socialism would end the abject poverty and social injustice he often encountered. *(Library of Congress)*

series of strikes, when workers refused to go to work and picketed a company or industry, swept the country. Between 1881 and 1905, the country witnessed 37,000 strikes involving almost seven million workers.

Working men and women were ready to demand fair pay and decent living conditions. Political activist Eugene Debs fired up unions with his speeches; union activist Big Bill Haywood faced company police while carrying a gun; anarchist Alexander Berkman shot and stabbed one of the country's strongest opponents of unions.

Most of the powerful, mainstream politicians in both parties catered to the wealthy and upper middle class. Most politicians ignored the obstacles faced by poor people who wanted to better themselves: their votes and campaign money came from businessmen and others with resources. This situation did not fit into Thomas's vision of how he wanted to spend his life, and he decided against a career in politics.

Instead, Thomas decided to enter the ministry. Maybe he could convince other members of the clergy and their parishioners that caring for others should be the first duty of the church. In 1908, he enrolled at Union Theological Seminary. To finance his education, he took a job with Christ Church in Manhattan, which bordered the rough-and-tumble neighborhood called Hell's Kitchen. While at Christ Church, he joined the Social Gospel movement, a group of clergy and lay men and women dedicated to working for a just society. Unlike many other Christian groups, the Social Gospel movement was focused on the here and now more than on the afterlife.

In 1910, Thomas met and fell in love with Frances Violet Stewart (called Violet). Violet had started a class at the church to teach people how to treat tuberculosis at home. It was the first class of its kind in the city. She also taught Sunday school with Thomas at Christ Church.

The Stewarts, a family of wealthy, conservative bankers, had doubts about Thomas as a husband for their daughter, who was petite, blue-eyed, well educated and traveled, and three years older than Thomas. He had little money and seemed to have little ambition to accumulate more. But he did have other assets—his social credentials, his academic record at Princeton, his handsome appearance and, most importantly, the fact that Violet loved him.

Thomas and Violet were married on September 1, 1910, and he began a new job as assistant to the pastor at the fashionable Brick Church on Fifth Avenue. He was nervous when he gave his first sermon, especially after he looked out on his wealthy audience of ladies in the latest hobble skirts, enormous hats, and high-button shoes, and the gentlemen in top hats and frock coats. But as he began to speak, his message overcame his nervousness. Using no notes, and gazing directly at the parishioners, he said the teachings of the church had delayed human progress for centuries. The poor and weak were told by the church to wait quietly until they are delivered to heaven, while the more fortunate were told not to worry about the poor because the poor will be blessed in the afterlife.

As he spoke, Thomas wondered what parishioners would say as they shook hands with him after the sermon. To his delight, many praised him, including Violet's grandfather. This was a turning point in his life. He now believed it might be possible to fulfill his vision of justice for all with the help of the church.

In his test for ordination, Thomas admitted he had doubts about the virgin birth and other miracles described in the Bible. He criticized the church, saying it should be more inclusive. Despite these admissions, he was accepted into the ministry and graduated from seminary in the spring of 1911 as the top student in his class.

With the birth of his son Norman Thomas Jr., it would have been prudent for him to choose a call to a wealthy and secure church. Instead, he chose to become pastor of the poverty-stricken East Harlem Church on 116th St. The congregation at East Harlem was a polyglot community of

Italians, Hungarians, Slovaks, and Swedes, many of whom spoke little or no English. The streets near the church were lined with peddlers of fish, salami, cheese, olive oil, and produce, and saloons were everywhere. The streets were crowded with stray cats, dozens of children with nothing to do but join rock-throwing street gangs who used garbage cans as shields.

The Thomas family moved to a three-story brick front. They sent coal to freezing parishioners and shoes to those who would otherwise go barefoot. They paid rent for families about to be evicted, sent nurses and doctors to those who needed medical attention, and tried to reason people away from drunkenness, prostitution, and crime. They formed church clubs for teenagers and started athletic programs and opened workrooms where the unemployed earned fifty cents a day making baskets. They worked hard and were convinced they were implementing the Social Gospel.

Before long there were two more children: William Stewart, born in 1912, and Mary Cecil, born in 1914. Thomas's in-laws built their daughter's family a nice house near Ridgefield, Connecticut. Although the gift troubled his conscience, Thomas accepted it. The large house was even more necessary when another daughter, Frances Beatrice, was born in 1915.

The church needed money and other resources. Thomas learned how to wheedle money from the rich to help the poor. Thomas and Violet worked as a team to convince doctors to reduce their charges, tenement landlords to postpone evictions, and funeral directors to lower prices. Thomas was optimistic that Harlem, and all other pockets of poverty, could be lifted into middle-class security. He saw selfishness and ignorance

This photograph shows a poverty-stricken mother and children in a New York City slum house. After graduating from college, Thomas began trying to help the poor through his job at a Presbyterian neighborhood center in Manhattan. *(Library of Congress)*

as the only obstacles. "I was of a generation of Americans . . . who had no doubt in progress." East Harlem Church grew steadily, increasing from fewer than five hundred members in 1911 to more than 1,500 in 1916.

The beginning of World War I in Europe, in August 1914, reawakened Thomas's interest in politics. The causes of the war included the emergence of Germany as a great world power, economic conflict created by the Industrial Revolution, and imperialism—the desire on the part of several nations to expand its territory and to control other parts of the world.

Thomas saw the war as a selfish struggle between rival imperialist states and was opposed to the United States entering the war.

When President Woodrow Wilson decided the United States should enter the war on the side of Great Britain and France in April 1917, Thomas joined an organization called the American Union against Militarism and the Fellowship of Reconciliation. The group had a Christian pacifist message, and he became head of the No Conscription League, which fought against the draft. He also spoke out against the war at every opportunity. Audiences responded to his message and thought he was magnetic, learned, and charming.

President Woodrow Wilson *(Library of Congress)*

Thomas received little support for his pacifist work from the church leadership. Some church members retaliated against him in petty ways. One parishioner said she would not donate Christmas candy and toys to parish children as long as Thomas was a church leader. Some parishioners did stick by him when he supported those who refused conscription on the grounds that war violated their moral beliefs.

His social vision was changing. Thomas asked himself if antiwar work was more important than parish work. His belief in Christian brotherhood was further eroded when an anti-German campaign spread across the nation. It encouraged scoffing at all things German, from sauerkraut to Dachshunds to Beethoven.

Thomas spoke from the pulpit about the failure of the church to meet its Christian obligation to promote peace. His superiors told him his message was hurting the church financially. By the fall of 1917, Thomas had to choose between maintaining his belief that the church should be pacifist or resigning from the church.

Thomas resigned the church to become the editor of the pacifist monthly magazine, *The World Tomorrow*. In articles published in the magazine, he accused the United States government of irresponsibility for taking part in a war, for discriminating against black soldiers, and for passing an unconstitutional espionage law. President Wilson wanted Thomas to be prosecuted as a violator of a new Sedition Law and sent him the message that "there is such a thing as indecent display of private opinions in public."

During the war, there were frequent assaults on freedom of speech. Politicians were whipping up public hysteria against antiwar activists. Sentences were handed out for alleged

This 1922 photo shows a young woman picketing outside the White House gates for amnesty for war protesters. *(Library of Congress)*

treason, and people were beaten for using anti-American expressions. One man was sentenced to ten years in prison for writing a letter against war profiteers and mailing it to a newspaper. A minister was horsewhipped for opposing hatred of Germans, and a German orchestra conductor was fired. The government publicized the names of sixty-two citizens in a list titled *Who's Who in Pacifism and Radicalism.* Thomas was on the list.

When the war ended in 1918, many U.S. politicians started a crusade against Communists and Socialists who, they said, wanted to destroy capitalism and the American way of life. There were also an increasing number of workers' strikes adding to the hysteria. About 6,000 people, many of them Socialists, were arrested on charges of treason, though most were found innocent.

Socialists thought that the capitalist economic system was the cause of the disparity of wealth as well as the war. They advocated for a system that limited private property and in which the essential services and businesses were owned by all the people and controlled by the government. This was not a widely popular belief, particularly among the powerful and politicians. The Socialist Party headquarters was trashed and party members were attacked. Thaddeus Sweet, the speaker of the New York State Assembly, declared that Socialist members of the Assembly had been elected "on a platform that is absolutely inimical to the best interests of the State of New York and the United States" and suspended legally elected Socialist legislators.

During the years after the war Thomas was busy with his ailing family, all of whom had contracted streptococcus infections that led to other problems. Violet was hospitalized several times because of heart problems. When his oldest son Tommy died of meningitis, Thomas was devastated.

Soon after Tommy's death, Thomas jumped back into his political work. He was disheartened that most Christians and their church leaders had supported President Wilson's suppression of civil liberties. Thomas came to believe he had no choice but to reject the religion of his father and resigned from the Fellowship for Reconciliation. He declared that he no longer believed in the Social Gospel. Now his hope for mankind lay in the hands of man, perhaps even in the hands of the Socialist Party, although it had dwindled from 108,000 members in 1912 to fewer than 27,000 by 1920.

Thomas started *The New Leader*, a daily labor-oriented paper. He wrote articles supporting workers' rights but did not always agree with union demands. In 1924, he accepted the Progressive Party's nomination for governor of New York, but instead of working on his own campaign he made speeches for an independent candidate for president, Senator Robert La Follette of Wisconsin. Thomas loved the excitement and the sway he held over an audience that came with speaking. He lost the election for New York governor, receiving only 99,000 votes, and La Follette also lost.

The next year, 1925, Thomas was nominated by the Socialist Party to run for mayor of New York City. He campaigned for better schooling, transportation, and housing but lost, earning only 40,000 votes to his opponent's 751,000 votes.

Thomas visited a coal mine where workers were on strike for higher wages. Management brought in replacement workers—the strikers called them scabs—to take the jobs of strikers. Violence escalated and martial law was imposed—strikers and sympathizers were commonly jailed. Thomas raised money to feed the strikers and cheered them on until he was charged with incitement to riot. He spent a night in jail before supporters paid his $10,000 bail. After four months, the mine workers gave up and went back to work—for lower wages.

In 1926, Thomas was nominated to be a candidate for New York state senator from the Lower East Side of New York City. Instead of concentrating on his own campaign, he spent most of his time promoting Socialist judge Jacob Panken's run for governor. The incumbent governor, Democrat Alfred Smith, and his party won in a landslide. In 1927, Thomas ran for New York City alderman and lost. This marked four consecutive years he had run and lost.

In 1928, Thomas accepted the Socialist Party nomination for president of the United States. Membership in the party was only 8,000 at that time. Violet's family financed most of his campaign against Republican Herbert Hoover and Democrat Al Smith. Knowing he had no chance of winning, Thomas focused on broadening the base of the Socialist Party by moving away from his former insistence on immediate nationalization of natural resources and industries. He received 267,000 votes; Hoover received 21,000,000 and Smith 15,000,000.

One year later, after the beginning of the Great Depression that left millions unemployed, he ran again as Socialist candidate for mayor of New York City. He again called for expansion and improvement of the transit system and for controls on rents. His opponents were formidable—popular Democratic Mayor Jimmy Walker and Republican Fiorella LaGuardia.

Thomas was told that many people would never vote for a Socialist because they feared socialism would lead to a Communist dictatorship. He tried to make socialism respectable by reminding voters that highways, schools, and water systems were publicly owned. His arguments may have helped—he received four times more votes than in 1925.

After the election, the economy continued to decline. Former business executives were unemployed and scuffling to put food on their family's table by selling apples or shining shoes—anything that would earn even the smallest income. New York City was full of boarded-up businesses, foreclosures, and sheriff's sales. As a member of the newly founded City Affairs Committee, Thomas pressured Mayor Walker, Governor Franklin Roosevelt, and President Herbert Hoover to create jobs and relief programs.

In 1930, Thomas ran for the U.S. Congress. At age forty-six, he was one of the most skillful speakers in the country and was known for what was called his million-dollar smile. Regardless, he lost another election.

In 1931, for the eighth consecutive year, Thomas ran for office and lost again, this time in a race for the presidency of the bureau of Manhattan. That loss, or the others, did not deter him from his vision. This defeat gave him the impetus to make an important decision: he turned away from the Presbyterian clergy. He became Mr. Thomas, and sometimes even Comrade Thomas, but no longer was he Reverend Thomas.

Thomas finally ran in an election he could win. He was voted a member of the executive committee of the Socialist Party. In this office he worked to make poverty a major concern. He said that in the city "men and women search the garbage cans . . . competing with rats and stray cats. . . . That's how the celebrated law of supply and demand works under capitalism." He believed the solution to poverty lay in the Socialist program of subsidizing consumers instead of producers and asked for emergency subsidies for the unemployed. This would lead to an increase in self-respect and better health for workers and their families. He supported public works, a shorter work week, agricultural relief, unemployment insurance, elimination of child labor, old age pensions, slum clearance, low-cost housing, higher taxes on corporations and the wealthy, and nationalization of basic industries.

Thomas's next run for election was for the presidency of the United States, in 1932. He received less than $50,000 in donations, while both Democrat Franklin Delano Roosevelt and Republican Herbert Hoover received millions of dollars. But as Thomas traveled throughout the country he was met by large crowds. In his speeches, he pointed out that twelve million people were unemployed and banks continued to close. "Before our eyes the Socialist prediction of the breakdown of capitalism is being fulfilled," he said.

Roosevelt won the election in a landslide. Some members of the Socialist Party tried to console Thomas by telling him that it was better to be right than to be president. Thomas said he wanted to be both.

In 1933, for the first time in nine years, Thomas did not run for office. He wanted to travel, to write, and to think. He also had speaking engagements booked up to a year in advance.

He took on causes all over the country for individuals as well as for large and small groups of workers. After visiting a cotton plantation in Arizona he complained the government was giving aid to employers, rather than to the sharecroppers who deserved it. While visiting shipyard workers in New Jersey, he supported their fight for fair wages and conditions. He led a march of 4,000 representatives of the unemployed in Washington, D.C. He spoke and wrote to hundreds of strikers, cornfield workers, textile workers, and state education councils. In all his speeches, he demanded a replacement of "the bogus democracy of capitalist parliamentarianism by a genuine workers' democracy."

In 1934, Thomas was nominated to run for the United States Senate. Despite heavy campaigning, he lost the election. Soon after the campaign he was on the road again. In Arkansas he helped tenant farmers fight against the powerful planters. He denounced the corporations being allowed to fire union members, and he publicized cases of union members being beaten, evicted from their homes, and sentenced to fines and imprisonment. In Mississippi, he was manhandled by police.

Thomas accepted an invitation to visit the White House. He tried to persuade President Roosevelt to accept his ideas

Franklin D. Roosevelt *(Library of Congress)*

for economic and social reform. Roosevelt did not agree or disagree; he asked Thomas to be patient. There was no time for patience, Thomas countered. The meeting with the president created trouble for Thomas when members of the old guard in the Socialist Party accused him of assuming too much authority.

Thomas predicted that 1936 would be a breakthrough year for socialism. He believed voters would oppose Roosevelt's reelection because employment had increased only 2.5 percent and corporate profit had increased by 36 percent since his election. He believed more Socialists would be elected in 1936 and 1938, thereby increasing his chances of becoming president in 1940.

Meanwhile, Thomas decided to run for governor of New York in 1938. He said, "I honestly feel the future of the Party is involved in making a showing in New York." However, he did not count on the backlash he received for his opposition to the U.S. involvement in the war that was on the horizon in Europe. Many Socialists and others on the left thought the U.S. should be more aggressive in trying to stop the spread of German Nazism and Italian Fascism. This disagreement splintered his potential base of voters, and Thomas ended up receiving fewer than 23,000 votes, less than in his run for mayor in 1925, and not even enough to keep the Socialist Party on the ballot in New York State.

When World War II began in Europe in 1939, Thomas demanded that the American Civil Liberties Union purge their membership of both communists and fascists or, at least ban them from leadership positions. Many people were surprised by this stance; for years, Thomas had insisted that all parties and religions should be equally respected.

Despite his resounding defeat in 1938, Thomas considered running for president in 1940. Perhaps he could form a new peace party. Then, in the spring of 1940, France fell to Adolf Hitler's German army, and Americans were less likely to support a peace candidate.

When the Socialist Party nominated him unanimously to run for president in 1940, however, Thomas accepted. He said it was his moral duty to run because no one else would. He inserted a noninterventionist plank in the party platform, saying that the United States should tell the world, "We will not share in the collective suicide of your wars." He received less than 1 percent of the votes.

After the election, Thomas admitted that he had blundered in dealings with Communists and other splinter groups. He had not worked hard enough to get farmers and labor support, and he had not accommodated the old guard of the Socialist Party. Perhaps, he mused, he was an idea man, not a politician.

Thomas continued to be an agitator for the causes he believed in. He demanded the release of political prisoners all over the world and worked against Hitler and the Italian dictator Benito Mussolini. He recruited volunteers to go to Spain to fight Francisco Franco, the fascist leader. He rejected the pleas of Socialist Party members who begged him to return to the single goal of gaining converts to pacifism.

When the Japanese attacked the United States Navy base at Pearl Harbor in Hawaii on December 7, 1941, Thomas announced that "our little Socialist Party has a great role to play in difficult days. . . . I see no escape from the choice: military success for the Axis or its enemies."

On December 11, the Federal Bureau of Intelligence

A photograph of Germans confined in an internment camp during WWII
(*Library of Congress*)

detained over 1,300 Japanese-Americans whom they classified, without any proof, as dangerous enemy aliens. In February 1942, the FBI designated twelve restricted areas in California, Oregon, and Washington as places to relocate the Japanese-Americans, who were not allowed to travel more than five miles away from their homes. In March, the United States government opened the first of several concentration camps where thousands of Japanese-Americans were forced to live. Two-thirds of the imprisoned were American-born citizens. They had to sell their homes and businesses for much less than they were worth. For most of the war they were detained at the isolated camps, in wooden barracks with only one room per family. Thomas opposed internment of the Japanese, insisting that civil liberties should never be curtailed, even in a time of war.

Thomas continued speaking and traveling. He also gave a weekly radio address. The Director of Public Safety in Jersey City refused to grant him a permit to hold an outdoor celebration of May Day and when Thomas defied the ban he was whisked away by police. The police put him on a ferry heading out of the city, but he got off the ferry, stepped onto a subway, and headed back to Jersey City. There, he went to the offices of a newspaper and made a statement about his treatment by the police. The office staff called the police, who removed him.

Although he was not advocating pacifism, he did support conscientious objectors—those who refused to participate in the war. It made little sense, he said, to persecute people for their beliefs, as thousands of Jews and others were being persecuted in Germany solely on the basis of what they believed. Thomas contacted the secretary of state to urge broad asylum in America for Jewish refugees, and he advocated sending food to starving nationals in countries occupied by the Nazis. He also carried on a running battle against racism in the U.S Army. When someone called him a defender of lost causes, Thomas corrected him: "*Not* lost causes—causes not yet won."

In his personal lifestyle, he remained the same Norman Thomas who had picked berries for a penny a quart, worked in a chair factory to help finance his college education, and worked in Hell's Kitchen to pay for his seminary studies. He was cautious about spending money. He wore old neckties to his simple office in a run-down building and rode second-class on public transportation.

In the 1944 election, for the fifth time in his life, Thomas ran for president. Predictably, his platform supported socialization of basic resources and an immediate peace offensive. He received only 80,000 votes, his worst vote total ever. President Roosevelt received 25,000,000 votes.

A few months after the election, Roosevelt died, and Vice-President Harry Truman assumed the office of president. When Truman ordered atomic bombs dropped on the Japanese cities of Hiroshima and Nagasaki, Thomas dedicated the rest of his life to preventing World War III. He advocated international disarmament and enforcement of human rights all over the world.

Thomas's wife, Violet, died of a heart attack in August 1947, at age sixty-six. In a letter to his children, Thomas wrote: "Just living with her and doing things together was fun. . . . She'd let me talk about problems and worries and often helped me by her shrewd common sense; she was loyal to the same ends but she never, thank God! turned home into another church meeting or Socialist debating society." The couple had been married thirty-seven years, and after Violet's death, Thomas told a friend, "The family has been very kind. So have my friends. But I am very lonely."

Thomas became even more involved in causes, perhaps to assuage his grief. In 1948, for the sixth time, he ran for president. He knew he could not win against either Truman or his opponent Republican Thomas Dewey, but he wanted to publicize his platform for peace.

Thomas lost faith in the prospect for a Socialist victory after the election. He believed the Socialist Party should concentrate on educating the electorate, not trying to capture an office.

After the war the tensions between the former allies, the United States and the Soviet Union, escalated. After a series

THE WHITE HOUSE

SEP 13 8 30 AM '48   September 11, 1948

RECEIVED

Hon. Harry S. Truman
The White House
Washington, D.C.

Dear President Truman:

This letter is not being written for publicity and will
not be released at any time. I am writing because I want to
tell you that I appreciate the firmness and patience with
which the governments of the United States and the other
Western nations have been conducting the negotiations about
Berlin, and because I want to bring to your attention some
remarks I shall deliver tonight at a dinner honoring Luigi
Antonini, Vice-President of the International Ladies' Garment
Workers Union.

In my talk I shall propose that the American government
put before the Paris United Nations General Assembly the
actions, in Berlin and elsewhere, by which the Soviet dictatorship menaces the peace of the world. I believe the Kremlin's
actions fall within the provisions of paragraph 2 of Article
II concerning the functions of the General Assembly.

I shall also suggest that the State Department confer with
all presidential candidates about referring the Berlin crisis
to the United Nations so that — as far as possible — our critical
relations with the Soviet Union may be taken out of the realm of
campaign politics.

Such a conference would put Henry Wallace on the spot. If
he did not go along, he would be even more isolated, and less
harmful to the United States, than he is now. If he goes along,
it will make things more difficult for Stalin.

In either case, it would demonstrate the essential unity of
all American non-Communist opinion against Soviet aggression and
would strengthen the chances of maintaining world peace.

I should appreciate hearing from you on your opinion
concerning this proposal.

Sincerely yours,

Norman Thomas

NT:hf

A copy of a letter Thomas sent to President Truman (*U.S. National
Archives, Truman Presidential Library*)

of near military conflicts in Berlin, Germany, and other areas, each government began charging the other of assuming too much power over other countries. This conflict came to be known as the Cold War. Under what came to be called the Truman Doctrine, the president declared, "I believe that it must be the policy of the United States to support free peoples who are resisting attempted subjugation." As U.S. troops began to be sent around the world to stop the expansion of communism, Thomas testified in Congress against American intervention in China, Indonesia, and Indochina.

Thomas was pleased when the United States signed the mutual defense treaty that created the North Atlantic Treaty Organization (NATO). This treaty stated that an attack on any one of the fourteen NATO countries would be considered an attack on all of them. He spoke against those who did not agree with the treaty. "The particular dissent which haunts me day and night is against the notion that peace for my children and grandchildren can be guaranteed by the present race in arms."

As a member of the American Federation of Labor and the Congress of Industrial Organizations (AFL-CIO), he toured Europe and North Africa to make a survey of labor's political and cultural groupings. He was concerned about human rights in half a dozen countries, including Peru, Sweden, the U.S., Uganda, Spain, and Yugoslavia. At all times and in every location, he reiterated his call for controlled universal disarmament.

About his religious beliefs, he said,

> I am no atheist. Indeed I am almost haunted by religion and often wish that I could regain the comfortable Christian theology

> of earlier years. I suppose the difference between me now and
> then [when I was young] could mostly be summed up by saying
> that then I expected more of both God and man than today. I
> think I like people rather better now than then partly because
> I expect less of them. And that goes for myself. Another thing
> that life seems to have taught me is . . . that fine moral and
> political generalizations have to be judged very often in terms
> of attainable goals.

At age seventy-seven, his health was failing, and his hearing faded. Arthritis put him on crutches part of the time. But his charm and integrity won over audiences throughout the country and the world.

Thomas was still active in dozens of organizations. He appeared before Congress to argue for equal radio-television time for minority candidates. He was thrilled with the Turn Toward Peace two-day demonstration of 4,000 college students from forty different states. Students carried signs: "Peace—The Cause That Refreshes" and "We Condemn Both U.S. and Soviet Testing" as they circled the White House in orderly ranks. Thomas said there was no logic in the program of President John F. Kennedy's administration. "It is like saying that if [kids] are fighting a lot at kindergarten, the thing to do is give them each a gun and say, 'There now, boys, go deter each other.'"

By 1966, Thomas was legally blind from retinal arteriosclerosis, and arthritis gnarled his body. He described himself: "I'm ancient, used-up and probably crazy." He still wrote (dictated) letters, read (listened to books on tape), and harassed politicians. He also slowly worked on an autobiography.

As a young man, Thomas had hoped that workers would be an agent for change. Now he admitted: "I do *not* believe that man is perfectible, to be honest with you. The best I can say that we are not damned by our gods or our genes to stay the way we are or the way we have been." He told an interviewer, "I like human beings. I'm very glad I'm one of them. But I think we're crazy. We're irrational. Look at our race prejudice, look at our inability to get out of the war, look at the crazy things we do in our personal lives."

When Norman Thomas died on December 19, 1968, a *New York Times* reporter wrote: "There are not many men in American public life who command greater esteem . . . than Norman Thomas."

NORMAN THOMAS

—⋖— timeline —⋗—

1884 Born on November 20 in Marion, Ohio.

1905 Graduates from Princeton; takes job at Presbyterian church in Manhattan.

1908 Enrolls in Union Theological Seminary; gets a job with Christ Church in Manhattan; joins the Social Gospel Movement.

1910 Marries Frances Violet Stewart.

1911 Graduates from seminary; ordained a minister; son, Norman Thomas Jr., born; accepts position as pastor of East Harlem church.

1912 Second child, William Stewart, born.

1914 Daughter, Mary Cecil, born.

1915 Second daughter, Frances Beatrice, born.

1917 Joins American Union Against Militarism and the Fellowship of Reconciliation; resigns from church.

1918 Becomes founding editor of pacific monthly, *The World Tomorrow*.

1920 Oldest child, Tommy, dies.

1923 Starts *The New Leader*, a daily labor-oriented paper.

1924 Runs unsuccessfully for governor of New York.

1925 Runs unsuccessfully for mayor of New York City.

1926 Loses race for New York Senate.

1927 Loses race for New York alderman.

1928 Runs unsuccessfully for president of the United States.

1929 Runs as Socialist candidate for mayor of New York City; again loses.

1930 Runs unsuccessfully for U.S. Congress.

1931 Defeated in race for the presidency of the bureau of Manhattan.

1932 Loses election for the presidency of the United States.

1934 Runs unsuccessfully for the U.S. Senate.

1938 Campaigns unsuccessfully for governor of New York.

1940 Makes yet another unsuccessful bid for the office of the U.S. presidency.

1944 Runs for president for a fifth time; loses to Roosevelt.

1947 Wife Violet dies of a heart attack.

1948 Runs for president a sixth time.

1968 Dies on December 19.

John Reed
(Library of Congress)

five

John Reed:

"I have always advocated revolution"

J ohn (Jack) Silas Reed was born in Cedar Hill, an ele-
gant area of Portland, Oregon, on October 22, 1887.
Jack later described his home as "a lordly gray mansion modeled on a French chateau, with its immense park,
its formal gardens, lawn, stables . . . and all the best that
money could buy." As a child, he was cared for by nurses
who kept him clean and tidy and out of mischief. A special
diet and medication eased some of the excruciating pain he
suffered from a chronic kidney problem. His playmates were
his brother Harry, two years younger, and a few other young-
sters who lived in the exclusive West End. A sculptor friend
described wealthy Portland society: "social life in Portland
was extremely closed and snobbish."

Always an avid reader, Jack's favorite stories could be
found in *The Arabian Nights*, a collection of ancient fairy tales,
fables, parables, and legends featuring characters such as Ali

Baba, Sinbad the Sailor, and Aladdin. Jack was a dreamer and a loner. One of his real-life heroes was his father, who was a crusader for President Theodore Roosevelt's battle for conservation of forest preserves.

Jack attended Portland Academy, a private school. He tried to build a tunnel between his home on King's Hill and the school, about one mile away. He thought he needed this to avoid any bullies who might try to steal his money as he walked to school. He admitted later, "My imagination conjured up horrible things that would happen to me if anybody hit me, and I simply ran away." His favorite pastimes were solitary—reading and writing poetry and prose. He did step out of his shyness enough to become a member of the editorial board of his school's literary magazine, *The Troubadour.*

At age sixteen Jack left for the Morristown School, a small elite academy in New Jersey. He was a tall, slender young man with an unruly shock of brown hair and intense brown eyes. Later he said of his years growing up in Portland: "I was neither one thing nor the other, neither altogether coward nor brave, neither manly nor sissified, neither ashamed nor unashamed. I think that is why my impression of my childhood is an unhappy one."

At Morristown, Reed distinguished himself by being outspoken. He defied school regulations by sneaking off into town in the evening to flirt with the young ladies. He knew he was handsome in his single-breasted jacket, high collar, wide necktie, and straw boater. The headmaster wrote of him: "Jack was a difficult and rather disturbing influence in the school." Jack wrote of himself: "I love beauty and chance and change. . . . I suppose I'll be a Romanticist."

The progressive movement, which sought to improve the well-being of everyone in American society, shaped much of Jack's early political opinions. The beginning of the twentieth century was a time of rapid economic and industrial growth. This growth brought with it a wide disparity in wealth and abuse of power, as well as a new generation of reformers. These reformers adopted the label "progressives" and included members of both major political parties. Progressives wanted to fight for workers' rights and force the government to protect the powerless and to provide for their health and safety. They also demanded equality and justice for blacks, women, foreign-born, and American Indians. They worked to reform voting regulations, educational opportunity, and public access to government officials. The journalists who were aligned with the progressives and wrote articles and books about the abuses committed by corporations and their allies in government were called muckrakers, a term to mean they "dug up all the dirt" they could find.

The Socialist Party under Eugene Debs was gaining converts for its platform of equal justice for the masses as Jack began attending Harvard University. This spirit of reform and dissatisfaction with the current state of affairs came to Harvard, where many of the student body of 4,000 turned their youthful enthusiasm to reform. The ferment, debates, and discussions appealed to Jack's intellectual curiosity. He loved the Saturday night meetings when he and his friends gathered in a crowded room lined from floor to ceiling with books, heated by a coal fire and lit by a single candle, to talk of political systems, philosophies, and recent books.

One of the issues that concerned them was the plight of immigrants, which had been dramatized in a best-selling novel by Upton Sinclair in 1906. *The Jungle* was an expose of the cruel treatment suffered by workers, mostly immigrants, in meat-packing plants.

Immigration continued unabated. In 1907 more than 1.2 million people came to the United States looking for jobs and opportunities. Instead, most found lives of poverty, squalor, and injustice.

Jack was not only focused on politics. He began writing and experimented with poetry and short fiction, and was published in the school magazine. One of his poems won a prize. From this, he gained some social acceptance, especially after his work was included in the prestigious *Harvard Monthly*.

Exhilarated with college life, Jack filled the pages of the *Harvard Lampoon* with humor. He poked fun at Harvard life, the instructors, Boston society, and himself. Many of his stories, poems, and plays focused on the need for reform. He wanted to enlist others in a struggle for women's suffrage, anti-Puritanism, sexual freedom, and atheism.

In 1910 Reed graduated from Harvard, much more confident than when he had entered. He told a journalist friend, Lincoln Steffens, that his goals were to make a million dollars, to get married and "to write my name in letters of fire against the sky." Steffens told him, "You can do anything you want to."

After graduation, Reed set sail on a cattle boat bound for Europe "for a year's happy-go-lucky wandering." In Paris he ate at good restaurants and hiked around France, reveling at the freedom from the pressures of college life. He also fell in love. He proposed to a French woman named Madeleine Filon. She accepted, and days later he set out for home, determined to earn a living for himself and his future bride.

Back in Portland, however, life was less than ideal. Reed's father had been defeated in his campaign to become a member of Congress, and his parents faced serious financial troubles. News of Reed's plan to wed only added to his parent's worries.

Reed then decided to leave Portland for New York City. There, he looked up his family's old friend, Steffens. Steffens knew Reed through his father, whom he had become acquainted with while reporting on a land fraud ring in Oregon, back in 1905. The senior Reed was a United States Marshal under U.S. president Theodore Roosevelt, and his efforts to end the fraud scheme left a deep, lasting impression on his idealistic son.

Reed's father had written to Steffens in New York, asking him to keep an eye out on Jack. "Get him a job, let him see everything, but don't let him be anything for a while," he wrote. "Don't let him get a conviction right away or a business or a career, like me. Let him play."

In 1911, at the age of twenty-three, Reed settled in Greenwich Village, a neighborhood in New York, where, Steffens said, culture took on the importance it should. Reed loved New York—the theaters, Chinatown, the skyscrapers and rivers, and the colorful lives of the recent immigrants. He wrote poem after poem extolling this new cosmopolitan world and joined groups that talked about art and writing and philosophy.

He described his new home:

> The swarming East Side—alien towns within towns—where the smoky flare of miles of clamorous pushcarts made a splendor of shabby streets; coming upon sudden shrill markets, dripping blood and fish-scales in the light of torches, the big Jewish

women bawling their wares under the roaring of great bridges, thrilling to the ebb and flow of human tides sweeping to work and back, west and east, south and north.

Reed also discovered the *Masses,* a publication read by rebels, anarchists, socialists, and feminists. The motto of the magazine was "Poems, stories and drawings, rejected by the capitalist press on account of their excellence, will find a welcome in this magazine."

Reed decided to become a professional writer. Steffens had recently left a job at the *American,* a magazine that published a variety of articles, short fiction, and poems. He helped Reed get a job on the staff.

Although he was paid very little, Reed was happy to be writing professionally. He wrote dozens of pieces—articles, satires, short stories, short fiction, humorous sketches—and learned to accept rejections without despairing.

Meanwhile, Reed broke off his engagement, saying that a man "could love and marry and be happy with any one of a thousand." Instead, he enjoyed a lively social life. He and his Harvard roommates and friends walked the streets of Manhattan at night or gathered in living rooms to discuss politics and philosophies. Some Americans were determined to press for radical changes in business, government, and social traditions. The Socialist Party with its focus on government ownership of natural resources and industry, as well as on the rights of workers to join unions, was gaining popularity.

All these ideas forced many people to rethink the American commitment to capitalism. President Woodrow Wilson enacted a graduated income tax. Anti-trust acts to limit the size of corporations and to guard against monopolies were introduced in the U.S. Congress. Black leaders talked openly against seg-regation in government employment. The prohibition of alcohol, women's suffrage, and stopping the United States from engaging in imperialism were often rancorously debated.

Reed wrote that New York was a magic city, but he was aware of the terrible living conditions in the ghettos and slums. The contrast between wealthy and poor was appalling. When he heard anarchist Emma Goldman debate the topic of socialism versus anarchism she appealed to his romantic instincts. He thought she showed that the life of a revolutionary could be both serious and joyful.

When his father died in the summer of 1912, Reed did some rethinking about life in the United States. Reviewing his father's life in politics, he came to believe that something was wrong with his country. "We have banded together to crush sensitiveness and fineness," he wrote. He blamed this on the emphasis on material success, which made everyone intent on building wealth and minimized the individual's responsibility to his community.

In New Jersey, 25,000 silk workers went on strike for an eight-hour day. Reed learned from William "Big Bill" Haywood, head of the Industrial Workers of the World (IWW), that a news blackout had kept reports of strikers being clubbed and jailed from being published. Reed went to New Jersey and walked the picket line with the striking men, women, and children.

At one point, seeking shelter from rain, Reed saw some strikers huddled on the porch of a company house near the mill. He climbed onto the porch with them and listened to their stories. Meanwhile, police arrived and ordered Reed and the strikers to "move on." Reed refused, saying "If I'm breaking any law, arrest me." The policemen arrested him and he spent four days in a filthy, unventilated cell. Reed said later he came to love his prison mates—tough boisterous men, mostly immigrants, who sang union songs and jeered at the jailers. Later at a mass rally he led the singing of the French national anthem "La Marseillaise" and the labor march "Internationale." He wrote a pageant on the strike that had one thousand workers in the cast. This pageant, and an article he wrote about a massacre of striking workers in Colorado, confirmed his commitment to political radicalism. His dreams of becoming a poet faded away.

In 1913, Steffens used his considerable influence as a muckraking journalist to get Reed an assignment reporting on the Mexican Revolution, in which revolutionaries were fighting for

A scene from the Mexican Revolution. During the Mexican Revolution, Reed joined the rebels that fought to overthrow the Mexican dictatorship. *(Library of Congress)*

Pancho Villa *(Library of Congress)*

control of the government. He wrote for both the *Metropolitan Magazine* and the New York *World*. In Mexico he met Pancho Villa, a Mexican rebel leader known for his Robin Hood style of taking from the wealthy to distribute to the peasants. Reed supported Villa's fight to overcome the dictatorship of Porfirio Diaz. He joined the rebels who fought with Villa and got to live the romantic myth of fighting for good over evil that he had admired in the *Arabian Nights* as a boy. He reported about Villa's soldiers: "Two thousand nondescript, tattered men, on dirty tough little horses, their serapes flying out behind, their mouths one wild yell. . . ." Highly respected reporter Walter

Lippmann said of Reed's stories that they were "the finest reporting that's ever been done."

Back in the United States, Reed collated his anecdotes, characters, and descriptions of Mexico in *Insurgent Mexico,* a book Lippmann called a "gorgeous panorama." Partly because of the publicity incited by Reed, the Mexican revolution became an issue worldwide.

Later in 1914, Reed went to Ludlow, Colorado, where hundreds of miners were on strike. After the strikers' camp was attacked and their tents set on fire, leaving twenty-six dead, Reed wrote "The Colorado War" and went on a speaking and writing crusade against the "Ludlow Massacre."

Reed's next assignment was as a foreign reporter for the *Metropolitan,* whose editors sent him to cover the European war that broke out in the summer of 1914. From Europe he reported: "And here are the nations, flying at each other's throats like dogs . . . and art, industry, commerce, individual liberty, life itself taxed to maintain monstrous machines of death." He also concluded that this was "not our war."

Reed wrote stories from England, Switzerland, Germany, and France. He recounted his experiences of walking through mud and corpses, "slogging along miles of soft, crooked trenches; tripping and pitching to the ground and being pulled along by friendly hands." In France, he borrowed a rifle from a German soldier who invited him to fire a couple of shots. Reed fired two shots in the general direction of the front line and gave the rifle back. It seemed innocent at the time, but this event later came back to haunt him.

Everywhere he saw bombed railroad stations, wrecked bridges, shuttered factories, and "long low mounds of earth that sometimes were the storage places of tons of beets, and sometimes graves—you couldn't tell which." He wrote that "War means an ugly mob-madness, crucifying the truth-tellers, choking the artists. . . . "

Moving on to Russia for several days, Reed experienced the same excitement he had felt in Mexico. "Russians themselves are, perhaps, the most interesting human beings that exist . . . Everyone acts just as he feels like acting, and says just what he wants to."

After four months in Europe he returned to the United States. Life in the states now seemed to be out of touch with reality. The *Metropolitan* wanted him to return to France as a correspondent, but his seemingly innocent incident with the German gun had been publicized, and the French government refused to accept him. He was sent to the Balkans instead.

As he waited to leave on assignment, Reed developed romantic ideas about the Balkans. "I'm sure I will like the people. It will be great to get on a horse and ride over mountain passes where Genghis Khan invaded Europe. I find that I am a celebrated figure already." While he awaited specific orders, Reed tried to convince audiences in the United States that the Germans did not commit wholesale atrocities and that England was partly culpable in causing the war.

When he arrived in the Balkans, Reed searched out musicians and writers and scholars. He was thrilled to discover and to write about the Serbian gypsies with their fiddles and bagpipes that accompanied every regiment, the peasant dancers leaping and strutting in their colorful costumes, and the singing and feasting at religious festivals. The Serb soldiers welcomed the U.S. soldiers as *pobratim*, or blood brothers.

He also found much corruption, heavy persecution of Jews, and a country "ripe for revolution."

Back in the United States, Reed decided to visit his mother in Portland. There, he met fellow writer Louise Bryant, who said she had fallen in love with him through his writing.

Bryant had been on a streetcar. "I began to read a story by Jack," she recalled. "I sat on the street car, passed my station not caring whether I ever reached my destination or not, and suddenly realized that I must have fallen in love

Louise Bryant

with somebody—whoever wrote that story." He described her as "an artist, a rampant, joyous individualist, a poet, and a revolutionary."

It didn't matter to Reed that Bryant was already married. He described her as "the first person I ever loved without reservation." A few weeks after their meeting, Bryant left her dentist husband and moved to New York to be with Reed.

In November of 1916, Reed had his long-ailing kidney removed. But before the surgery, he insisted on marrying Bryant, who had obtained a divorce from her husband.

That same year the company Scribner's published his book *The War in Eastern Europe*, a collection of seven long articles he had written for the *Metropolitan*. The work is full of Reed's admiration for peasants and workers, scorn for politicians, and suspicion of the wealthy. Despite his admiration for peasants, though, he bemoaned their lack of intelligence and vision.

As U.S. intervention into the European war looked imminent, Reed became a popular speaker. He called for a halt to preparedness for war. He insisted that business interests were trying to frighten the country into patriotism. He called on audiences to be aware of the business advantages of contracts with large steel companies for armor and armor-plating, shipbuilders, and the investment companies that supported them. He also foresaw a potential U.S. empire of capitalists which would take advantage of underpaid labor at home to furnish the war. "[The American laborer] will do well to realize that his enemy is not Germany, nor Japan; his enemy is that 2 percent of the United States who own 60 precent of the national wealth," he said. In the presidential election of 1916 he found it easy to support Democratic incumbent President Woodrow Wilson who promised not to send troops to the war in Europe.

The following March President Wilson put guns and naval crews on merchant ships. On March 18, three United States vessels were sunk in the Atlantic. Editors told Reed that he must temper his beliefs against the war. He chose not to accept assignments. Emotionally overwrought and strapped by lack of money, Reed retreated into a kind of isolation, open only to Bryant and to his writing, in which he was able to say exactly what he meant. He described the future: "Within a very few months now the casualty lists will be appearing. . . . Our streets will slowly fill with pale figures in uniform, leaning on Red Cross nurses; with men who have arms off, hands off, faces shot away, men hobbling on crutches, pieces of men." In Europe, country after country joined the war effort.

In 1917, President Wilson asked the U.S. Congress to declare war on Germany and its allies. Suddenly, the atmosphere in the United States was highly patriotic. Americans were arrested and sent to prison for opposing the war, and radical newspapers, including *The Masses*, were banned. Reed wrote: "I must find myself again. Whenever I have tried to become some one thing, I have failed . . . only by drifting with the wind have I found myself."

In August of 1917, Reed and Bryant decided to travel to Russia to witness the revolution. But no editor wanted to sponsor this well-known anti-war activist whose writing had irritated so many readers. Finally, a friend convinced a wealthy Socialist to finance the trip. He reported for the Socialist New York *Call* and the magazine *Seven Arts*, while

Bryant reported for a press syndicate. Reed hoped he would witness the people overturning their longtime rulers and the ruling class in order to create a new and just society.

In St. Petersburg, Reed went to meetings of many diverse groups that were held in barracks, factories, streets, and meeting halls. He saw the Winter Palace, one of the ruling family's homes, being defended by student officer candidates from the growing crowd of hungry and angry citizens. In Moscow, he witnessed the architectural damage to the monuments of the Kremlin, and the chaos of wounded soldiers returning from the front lines. He wondered why Tsar Nicholas II did not try to respond to his people's needs.

Although he was officially a journalist, Reed also represented the American Socialist Party. Ever a romantic, he wrote to a friend: "We are in the middle of things and believe me, it's thrilling. For color and terror and grandeur this makes Mexico look pale." When a fellow reporter protested that his reporting was neither objective nor factual, Reed said he would not write with detachment, as reporters are supposed to do. For Reed, liberation came from the heart as well as from the head.

He took a trip through Russia, traveling fourteen hours in a third-class coach across the wheat plains of the steppe to the front lines of the brutal war. His first look at a Russian military camp evoked images of the romantic Russia he had read about in folk tales.

However, he received a rough surprise when, instead of the welcome they expected, he and his fellow reporters were seized by the Russian military and held captive in a tiny hotel room. They were refused any communication with the outside world. Quickly their goal changed from describing the Russia they saw to getting out of the country as fast as possible. After a couple of weeks in captivity they were allowed to go free while they waited for permission to leave the country. The men enjoyed themselves thoroughly as guests in private homes, with food and liquor flowing, and having conversations about everything from the war to peasant uprisings to sex. Reed wrote: "Russian ideas are the most exhilarating, Russian thought the freest, Russian art the most exuberant . . . and the Russians themselves are perhaps the most interesting human beings that exist." He was not unaware of the political and military tyranny, injustice and corruption of the czarist regime, but he believed all that could change.

After several weeks, they were allowed to leave for Romania and Bulgaria. Exhausted from traveling, Reed returned to the United States in late April 1918 to settle down—at least temporarily. Bryant had returned months earlier.

Meanwhile, in Russia, the war and the suffering it caused brought on the final breakdown of the already inadequate social services, which paved the way for a revolution of the people. First there was a revolution led by populist and liberal members of the Russian parliament, called the Duma. But when these leaders refused to take Russia out of the war the people's angst returned. Communist leaders such as Vladimir Lenin and Leon Trotsky then convinced the crowds that they could take over the country, end the war, and build a just and equitable Communist state. The Bolshevik (a word loosely translated as majority) Party, led by Lenin, seized power and began a Communist experiment in social reorganization.

The romantic idealist in Reed was enchanted with the potential of an awakened workingman in Russia. He resolved to go back to Russia and asked Bryant, who was working

Vladimir Lenin speaking to a crowd of supporters

as a freelancer in France, to meet him there. The summer before he left, Reed completed an essay, "Almost Thirty," in which he characterized himself as restless, scattered in ambition, and losing his vitality. The mini-autobiography tells of a man who is constantly driven by his moods and enthusiasms, short-lived though they are. "I love beauty and chance and change, but less now in the external world and more in my mind."

Reed arrived in Russia before the Bolshevik takeover. The country was in mass confusion. Citizens were revolting against high prices, short rations, and unequal distribution of land—and the war. Spontaneous organizations of workers, peasants, and soldiers clashed with each other and the police. The police were dysfunctional. Talk of an imminent German invasion added to the fear and confusion.

Reed had studied the philosophy of Marxism and understood the forces that motivated the Communist revolutionists, but his heart soon took over his head and he was caught up in the romance of the movement. He determined to write about the spirit of the revolution as well as the events.

In Viborg, Russia, Reed helped lead a mass protest of 6,000 workers angered by the United States' indictment of Emma Goldman and Alexander Berkman for speaking against the war. The U.S. embassy in Russia denounced Reed as a spy and traitor.

For five months he attended hundreds of meetings and observed speeches, proclamations, troop movements, skirmishing, and uprisings. Then the unrest escalated. Masses of armed soldiers and workers crowded onto the streets and broke into stores and businesses, and looted palaces and government buildings. He watched as workers took over factories, railroad stations, telegraph companies, telephones, and post office buildings.

Reed thought this was more than a war between haves and have-nots. He wrote that the uprising of the masses and workingman was a model of democratic action.

In November the Bolsheviks seized power in St. Petersburg. He was in the crowd when Lenin announced: "Now begins a new era in the history, and this third Russian Revolution must finally lead to the victory of Socialism."

Feverish with excitement, Reed tried to be everywhere and to write about it with incredible speed. He took voluminous notes. He was convinced he was witnessing his long-held dream of a successful workers' uprising.

In addition to his journalistic work, he joined the new

Bureau of International Revolutionary Propaganda to help issue flyers and newspapers encouraging the German troops to overthrow the German Kaiser and to work for socialism in their country as the Russians were doing. He assumed the title of Commissar of Art and Amusement and promised himself and anyone who would listen that he would produce fireworks, festivals, and orchestra concerts for the people. He was apparently unaware of how severe and widespread starvation and homelessness were in Russia. He insisted that joyous celebrations were an essential part of a revolution.

Reed found a partner to help put out a daily newspaper in St. Petersburg, which had been renamed *Petrograd*. The paper reflected his belief that Russia would become a truly democratic socialist state with all natural resources, factories, banks, and land controlled by the government for the betterment of everyone.

Despite all the excitement, the fact that he had become a committed Bolshevik, Reed wanted to return to the United States. He was a reporter with a world-shaking story to write. There were problems in trying to get back, though. He had been accused of being a traitor before he left the U.S. and was even more suspect after writing several articles extolling the Russian Revolution and criticizing the United States for not helping the workers and peasants. He feared American officials would confiscate the huge collection of documents and other papers he had collected in Russia. Reed asked Leon Trotsky, one of the Bolshevik leaders, to help him. Trotsky named Reed the Soviet Consul to New York, which gave him diplomatic immunity from any action by the United States government.

The consulship was canceled when a U.S. ambassador

warned the Russians that Reed was untrustworthy. Still, he was allowed to take his papers freely through customs when he left Russia.

When Reed finally landed in the states, on the morning of April 28, 1918, his papers were confiscated, and he was strip-searched and held for questioning. To all questions he gave the same answer: "I am a Socialist and I am going to engage in Socialistic work within the law." He was allowed to go free but was told that his papers would be held until it was determined if they contained anything contrary to the interests of the United States government.

After a warm welcome from his supporters, Reed fell into despondency. Without his papers, he said, "I am unable to write a word of the greatest story of my life, and one of the greatest in the world." He was arrested in Philadelphia for speaking on the street and charged with inciting to riot. Lincoln Steffens encouraged him to write but to not try to publish because it could not possibly be accepted in the current climate. Reed responded that this was the best time to publicize the truth. "All movements have had somebody to start them, and, if necessary, go under for them."

The United States was still at war and consumed with anti-German hysteria. Bans were placed on teaching the German language in schools and German music and performers were boycotted. German-Americans were persecuted, and so-called patriots harassed citizens whom they considered to be disloyal. Because Socialists had spoken against the war, they were also persecuted. Their headquarters were raided in many cities.

Throughout the summer, Reed tried unsuccessfully to get his papers released. He had not been charged with a crime. He had to turn to speaking as a means of making money. One of his main messages was that the United States should recognize the Bolsheviks as a government formed by visionaries who were creating a democratic and just society. He often opened his speeches addressing the audience as *Tovarischi,* the Russian word for comrades. The speeches brought him both applause and criticism. They also brought charges of inciting to riot, and several times he had to pay fines to stay out of jail. In some places his luggage was confiscated. In Cleveland officials told him, "You can't eat your dinner in a restaurant, you can't go to the theater, you can't lay down to sleep, without we hear every word you utter."

When Allied troops landed in Siberia in Eastern Russia to try to overthrow the Communist Revolution, Reed spoke out against it. He was accused of being disloyal, arrested, and freed on $5,000 bail. Then propaganda was issued that claimed several Bolshevik leaders were secret agents of the German government. The staff of the *Masses* was charged with conspiracy to violate the Espionage Act. Reed was arrested for the headline of an article he had written citing the emotional damage done to soldiers by war. The title of the article was "Knit a Strait-Jacket for Your Soldier Boy." After the trial, seven of the jury voted for conviction and five for no conviction. Reed was freed.

On November 11, 1918, the Germans surrendered. The war had left the social structure of Europe on the brink of disaster.

Reed's Russian notes were finally returned to him, but it was too late to fulfill the contract he had for his book. They had canceled it because the book was sympathetic toward Russia and communism, and the company did not want to get on the wrong side of the government.

Undeterred, Reed set out to write his story. In two months of furious writing he produced *Ten Days that Shook the World.* Written in a highly dramatic style, the book chronicles the coming of the Bolshevik revolution, the revolution itself, and its after-affects. There is no individual hero in this story. The hero is the masses of men who, in Reed's eyes, only seek power and freedom for the oppressed and underprivileged. Vivid descriptions of events, eloquent speakers, and the doubts and fears of workers come to life in simple, powerful words. The work is a clearly biased summary of Reed's feelings about the revolution, which had restored his faith in the working class.

When people asked Reed if a revolution like the one in Russia could happen in the United States he was quick to answer that it could not. He said a revolution demanded an educated working class with a feeling for history and a vision for the future, and the workingman in the United States America did not have these qualities. He also said the Socialist Party did not have the capacity to create a revolution.

Reed was popular in the Socialist Party, but he remained an individualist and was uncomfortable in organizations. His role as interpreter of the Russian revolution gave him great prominence in the party, however.

Reed helped draft a manifesto for a formal Left Wing umbrella organization and became its International Delegate. He also became editor of a weekly publication, the New York *Communist.* To many people, the words Bolshevik and Communist would soon become synonymous with the words repression and totalitarianism, and they would link both words to the word socialism. It was an easy step because both theories supported stronger government controls. Anti-communistic and anti-socialistic movements grew and strengthened.

As Americans were freed of wartime restrictions such as the no-strike pledge, U.S. workers became involved in more than 3,600 strikes with more than half a million workers in 1919. As strikes spread across the country, fear rose that labor troubles would bring the country to the brink of revolution.

Tales of real and imagined Bolshevik horrors were repeated and exaggerated. Stories of all educated men being murdered and thousands of women being raped and other acts of brutality and cruelty spread around the country and were publicized by politicians and the media. To counter the stories, Reed and Bryant volunteered to testify before a Congressional committee. During his testimony, Reed was asked if he advocated a Bolshevik-type revolution in America. He answered, "I have always advocated a revolution in the United States. . . . By revolution I mean profound social change. I do not know how it is to be attained." Despite insistent questioning, he refused to admit that social change must be accompanied by force.

The outcome of the hearing was a report that Bolshevism was the greatest danger facing the United States and that stringent legislation was necessary to combat the threat. Reed would not sit still and watch the Communist Party in the U.S. lose its fight for relevance. He believed the fledgling party needed the recognition of the Communist International. He knew that he would be the best representative to ask for this recognition.

Reed traveled to Moscow, the new Soviet capital, and presented the Executive Committee of the Communist International with the formal request for international recognition for the Communist Party of the United States. The International leaders promised to study the matter.

While Reed waited in Moscow he had a chance to study the effects of the Russian Revolution. He had conversations with Soviet leader Vladimir Lenin, who highly approved of *Ten Days that Shook the World*. Reed also found poverty and despair among the peasants, who were rapidly losing faith in communism. He also discovered that the Cheka, the Soviet secret police, were waging a reign of terror in an attempt to stamp out all dissension before it could harm the movement toward communism.

In early February 1920, Reed planned to go back to the United States, although he knew he would face a trial on charges of criminal anarchy. In Finland, on the way home, he was charged with smuggling diamonds because he was carrying jewels to sell and raise money to help the Communist Party in America. He was imprisoned, and the United States government asked Finland to keep him in jail. He was kept in solitary confinement and allowed out of his cell just once a day for a short walk. After three months he wrote to Bryant: "I have nothing to read, nothing to do. I can only sleep about five hours and so am awake, penned in a little cage, for nineteen hours a day."

Reed was released the first week in June. Bryant had warned him that the political climate of the United States would be intolerable, so he returned to Russia. He was welcomed in Russia, where he tried to heal his body and spirit. He appreciated the changes that had been made to make Russia a more livable place. He wrote that all was not yet well in Soviet Russia, but he believed the country was heading toward a better life for all under communism.

He attended the Second Congress of the Communist International in July 1920. In the midst of this group Reed felt some of the romantic fulfillment he had when he first traveled to Russia. He appointed himself an unofficial welcomer and met people who had smuggled themselves into the country.

For Reed, a strong negative aspect of the congress was the self-interest of its leaders, who seemed to think more of their political status than for the workers they were supposed to represent. Intra-party debates abounded, weakening the solidarity he hoped would come from the congress. He tried to explain the United States' position on communism, but the meeting attendees were largely critical and voted that "the revolutionary proletariat considers the position of our American comrades absolutely incorrect."

On September 15, 1920, Bryant came to visit him. Perhaps partly to protect herself and the man she was having an affair with from arrest, she begged Reed not to return to the United States. Although they did some touring together, Reed was nervous and anxious to get on with his writing. He wanted to finish a second volume about the Russian Revolution and then begin a novel that had been on his mind for years.

Then Reed suddenly fell ill with typhus, a disease for which doctors could do little. Before long he could barely swallow. As his body wasted away he was wracked with pain. He drifted in and out of hallucinations until he died, on October 17, 1920.

Reed's body lay in honor for a week in the Temple of Labor as visitors filed past to pay homage. He was buried in front of a walled brick citadel beside the remains of ancient kings and martyrs. Over his grave waved a banner that read, "The leaders die, but the cause moves on."

John Reed was a poet, playwright, and journalist. He was a romantic first and a revolutionary second. He said, "On the whole, ideas alone don't mean much to me. I had to see . . . it didn't come to me from books that the workers produced all the wealth in the world, which went to those who did not earn it." He saw his mission clearly:

> All I know is that my happiness is built on the misery of others, so that I eat because others go hungry, that I am clothed when other people go almost naked through the frozen cities in winter, and that fact poisons me, disturbs my serenity, makes me write propaganda when I would rather play.

For all his missteps and romanticism, Reed was always true to his vision. In the process he made many people think about war and injustice and the responsibility of those who are fortunate to share with the less fortunate to build a better world.

JOHN REED

—◆— timeline —◆—

1887 Born October 22, 1887, in Portland, Oregon.

1904 Leaves home to attend Morristown School in
New Jersey.

1910 Graduates from Harvard; sets sail for Europe.

1911 Settles in Greenwich Village in New York City.

1913 Reports on Mexican Revolution for *Metropolitan*
magazine.

1914 Leaves United States for Europe to cover World War I
for *Metropolitan* magazine; *Insurgent Mexico*
published.

1915 Meets fellow writer Louise Bryant while visiting
mother in Portland.

1916 Marries Bryant; long-ailing kidney removed;
Scribner's publishes his book *The War in
Eastern Europe*.

1917 Travels with Bryant to Russia to witness the revolution.

1918 Returns to U.S.; begins speaking tour.

1919 *Ten Days that Shook the World,* his chronicle
of the Bolshevik revolution, published; travels to
Moscow to get recognition for Communist Party of
the United States; befriends Soviet leader
Vladimir Lenin.

1920 Dies October 17 in Russia of typhus; buried with
kings and Bolshevik martyrs beside the Kremlin wall.

Sources

EUGENE DEBS

p. 11, "beloved little community . . ." Nick Salvatore, *Eugene V. Debs: Citizen and Socialist* (Urbana: University of Illinois Press, 1982), 3.

p. 14, "enter upon a more righteous . . ." Ibid., 28.

p. 14, "Does the brotherhood . . ." Ginger, *A Biography*, 38.

p. 17, "keen sense of humiliation . . ." Eugene V. Debs, "The Secret of Efficient Expression," *Coming Nation*, July 8, 1911.

p. 17, "big drops of cold sweat. . . " Ibid.

p. 17, "I bought an encyclopedia . . ." Ibid.

p. 19, "not for the purpose..." Ginger, *A Biography*, 79.

p. 23, "The first shots fired . . ." Ibid., 153.

p. 24, "I appeal to you to be men . . ." Ibid., 155.

p. 25, "rests with the people themselves . . ." Ibid., 172.

p. 25, "I am a Populist . . ." Ibid., 167.

p. 26, "The issue is Socialism versus Capitalism . . ." Ibid., 209.

p. 27, "He is a true disciple of Jesus Christ ." Ibid., 285.

p. 28, "The end of class struggles . . ." Ibid., 252.

p. 29, "You are the greatest . . ." Ray Ginger, *Eugene V. Debs: A Biography* (New York, Collier Books, 1949), 258.

p. 29, "As individual wage slaves . . ." Ibid., 25.

p. 29, "ignorant, lazy, unclean . . ." Ibid., 277.

p. 30, "I think the outlook . . ." Ibid., 325.

p 31, "You should have no more . . ." Ibid., 345.

p. 31, "Any nation that today . . ." Ibid., 346.

p. 35, "I will be a candidate at home . . ." Ibid., 418.

p. 36, "It is he [Wilson} . . ." Ibid., 426.

p. 37, "You cannot seem to understand ..." Ibid., 431

p. 38, "Socialism will never die . . ." Ibid., 466.

p. 38-39, "As a locomotive fireman . . ." Ibid., 33.

EMMA GOLDMAN

p. 43, "As long as I could think . . ." Emma Goldman, vol. 1, *Living My Life* (New York: Alfred A. Knopf, Inc., 1931), 59.

p. 46, "Girls do not have to learn . . ." Alix Shulman, *To the Barricades: The Anarchist Life of Emma Goldman* (New York: Thomas Y. Crowell Company, 1971), 32.

p. 46, "Ah, there she was . . ." Goldman, *Living My Life*, vol. 1, 11.

p. 46, "She held her torch . . ." Ibid.

p. 46, "We, too, Helena and I . . ." Ibid.

p. 46-47, "gruff voices . . . roughly pushed us," Ibid.

p. 48, "at the mercy of a few . . ." Shulman, *To the Barricades*, 43.

p. 49, "With one leap . . ." Goldman, *Living My Life*, vol. 1, 10.

p. 50, "I had a distinct sensation . . ." Ibid.

p. 52, "something strange happened . . ." Shulman, *To the Barricades*, 73.

p. 53, "It sounded the awakening . . ." Goldman, *Living My Life* , vol. 1, 84.

p. 57, "Frick was the symbol . . ." Emma Goldman, vol.1, *Living My Life* (1931: Anarchy Archives, 1995), http://dwardmac.pitzer.edu/ANARCHIST_ARCHIVES/ goldman/living/living1_11.html (accessed February 26, 2007), 1:8.

p. 54, "Sasha's act would be . . . " Ibid.

p. 54, "Sasha is giving . . . " Ibid.

p. 55, "beautiful comradery," Ibid., 1:11.

p. 55, "Demonstrate before the palaces . . ." Shulman, *To the Barricades*, 95.

p. 56, "The State of New York . . ." Ibid., 103.

p. 57, "Every fibre of her being . . ." Wexler, *An Intimate Life*, 85.

p. 60, "I am like the incurable drunkard . . ." Ibid., 119.

p. 60, "a pioneer spokesman...." Shulman, *To the Barricades*, 136.

p. 60, "The struggle is going on . . ." Ibid., 139.

p. 62, "Hanging is none too good . . ." Ibid., 153.

p. 62, "powerful country [was] moving . . ." Ibid., 145.

p. 63, "If it is a crime . . ." Ibid., 170.

p. 64, "For such people as would . . ." Ibid., 184.

p. 65, "I have my one Great Love," Alice Wexler, *Emma Goldman: An Intimate Life.* (New York: Pantheon Books, 1984), 247.

p. 65, "Be of good cheer . . ." Ibid., 186.

p. 65, "if every rebel were sent . . ." Ibid., 193.

p. 65, "no one need to worry . . ." Wexler, *An Intimate Life*, 247.

p. 66, "I protest against these proceedings," Shulman, *To the Barricades,* 195.

p. 66, "promise and hope of the world," Ibid., 204.

p. 66, "I must raise my voice . . ." Ibid., 213.

p. 68, "Men have come and gone . . ." Ibid., 222.

p. 69, "Did it not occur to you . . ." Wexler, *An Intimate Life*, xviii, xix.

p. 69, "bow to nothing except . . ." Ibid., 281.

p. 69, "My life —I had lived . . ." Goldman, *Living My Life*, vol. 2, 993.

p. 69, "in many of my more important . . ." Shulman, *To the Barricades*, 235.

UPTON SINCLAIR

p. 74, "My Cause is the Cause . . ." Petri Liukkonen, "Upton Beall Sinclair," Books and Writers, http://www.kirjasto.sci.fi/sinclair.htm (accessed February 26, 2007).

p. 75, "My life was a series . . ." Leon Harris, *Upton Sinclair: American Rebel* (New York: Thomas Y. Crowell Company, 1975), 10.

p. 75, "always I wore tight shoes . . ." Upton Sinclair, *The Autobiography of Upton Sinclair* (New York: Harcourt, Brace & World, Inc., 1962), 30.

p. 75, "I was an extraordinarily devout . . ." Harris, *American Rebel*, 12.

p. 77, "I kept my little notebook . . ." Ibid., 25.

p. 77, "Old Lady: You look . . ." Jon A. Yoder, *Upton inclair* (New York: Frederick Ungar Publishing Co., 1975), 21.

p. 77, "I kept two secretaries..." Liukkonen, "Upton Beall Sinclair."

p. 77, "The burden of my spirit . . ." Sinclair, *The Autobiography,* 70.

p. 77-78, "were nothing but a bait . . ." Harris, *American Rebel*, 168.

p. 78, "You were given to me . . ." Ibid., 41.

p. 78, "I bow in joy . . . " Ibid.

p. 78, "I did not have to carry . . ." Yoder, *Upton Sinclair*, 24.

p. 81, "Did I wish to know . . ." Spartacus Education, "Upton Sinclair," http://www.spartacus.schoolnet.co.uk (accessed February 26, 2007).

p. 82, "I advise without hesitation . . ." Ibid.

p. 82, "I aimed at the public's heart . . ." Yoder, *Upton Sinclair*, 40.

p. 5, "radical action must be taken . . ." Spartacus Education, "Upton Sinclair."

p. 83, "not one atom of any condemned . . ." Yoder, *Upton Sinclair*, 42.

p. 83, "Never have I been . . ." Ibid., 45.

p. 85, "nothing but legalized slavery," Harris, *American Rebel*, 116.

p. 86, "I feel that my life . . ." Ibid., 139.

p. 86, "I intend this night . . ." Ibid., 144.

p. 87, "When I see a line . . ." Spartacus Education, "Upton Sinclair."

p. 89, "I believe in the present . . ." Ibid.

p. 89, "if Germany be allowed to win . . ." Ibid.

p. 89, "I grant every man . . ." Harris, *American Rebel*, 163.

p. 98, "Any stigma . . ." Massachusetts Foundation for the Humanities, "Mass Moments: Massachusetts Executes Sacco and Vanzetti. August 23, 1927," http://www.massmoments.org/moment.cfm?mid=245 (accessed February 26, 2007).

p. 92, "The results were amazing . . ." Sinclair, *The Autobiography*, 245.

p. 93, "There was a time . . ." Harris, *American Rebel*, 326.

p. 93, "I know I can accomplish . . ." Ibid., 273.

p. 95, "What beat us . . ." Ibid., 320.

p. 95, "I wrote [*Dragon's Teeth*] with tears . . ." Yoder, *Upton Sinclair*, 12.

p. 96, "I had what was estimated . . ." Sinclair, *The Autobiography*, 304.

p. 96, "I'm sure I'm marrying one . . ." Harris, *American Rebel*, 352.

p. 96-97, "I believe what I have believed . . ." Sinclair, *The Autobiography*, 329.

NORMAN THOMAS

p. 102, "Yankee carpetbagger," W.A. Swanberg, *Norman Thomas: The Last Idealist* (New York: Charles Scribners' Sons, 1976), 5.

p. 103, "We stuck together . . ." Ibid., 9.

p. 104, "on a broken chair . . ." Dwight Steward, *Mr. Socialism* (New Jersey: Lyle Stuart, Inc., 1974), 69.

p. 104, "Social justice makes better men." Thomas, *Socialism Re-examined*, 210.

p. 104, "Poverty was very great . . ." Murray B. Seidler, *Norman Thomas: Respectable Rebel* (New York: Syracuse University Press, 1961), 12.

p. 109, "I was of a generation . . ." Swanberg, *The Last Idealist,* 39.

p. 111, "there is such a thing . . ." Steward, *Mr. Socialism,* 118.

p. 113, "on a platform that is absolutely inimical . . ." Swanberg, *The Last Idealist*, 79.

p. 116, "men and women search . . ." Ibid., 134.

p. 117, "Before our eyes . . ." Steward, *Mr. Socialism,* 144.

p. 117, "the bogus democracy . . ." Swanberg, *The Last Idealist,* 167.

p. 119, "I honestly feel the future . . ." Ibid., 228.

p. 120, "We will not share . . ." Seidler, *Respectable Rebel*, 208.

p. 120, "our little socialist Party . . ." Swanberg, *The Last Idealist*, 259.

p. 122, "*Not* lost causes . . ." Ibid., 279.

p. 123, "Just living with her . . . " Ibid., 307.

p. 123, "The family has been . . ." Ibid.

p. 125, "I believe that it must be . . ." James West Davidson and Mark H. Lytle, *The United States* (New Jersey: Englewood Cliffs), 637.

p. 125, "The particular dissent which . . ." Swanberg, *The Last Idealist, 328.*

p. 125, "I am no atheist. . . " Ibid., 367.

p. 126, "It is like saying . . . " Ibid., 460.

p. 126, "I'm ancient, used-up . . ." Swanberg, *The Last Idealist,* 476.

p. 126-127, "I do *not* believe that man . . ." Ibid., 472.

p. 127, "I like human beings..." Ibid., 464.

p. 127, "There are not many men . . ." Ibid., 329.

JOHN REED

p. 131, "a lordly gray mansion . . ." Richard O'Connor and Dale Walker, *The Lost Revolutionary* (New York: Harcourt, Brace & World, Inc., 1967), 4.

p. 131, "social life in Portland . . ." Rosenstone, *Romantic Revolutionary,* 7.

p. 132, "My imagination conjured up . . ." Ibid., 19.

p. 132, "I was neither . . ." Ibid., 5.

p. 132, "Jack was a difficult . . ." Ibid., 26.

p. 132, "I love beauty . . ." John Reed, *Ten Days That Shook the World* (New York: The Modern Library, 1920), 260.

p. 134, "to write my name . . . " Ibid., xiv.

p. 134, "You can do anything," Ibid.

p. 134, "for a year's . . ." Charles A. Madison, Critics and Crusaders: A Century of American Protest (New York: Frederick Ungar Publishing Co., 1947), 508.

p. 135, "Get him a job . . ." O'Connor and Walker, *The Lost Revolutionary,* 50.

p. 135-136, "the swarming East Side . . ." Rosenstone, *Romantic Revolutionary,* 79.

p. 136, "Poems, stories, and drawings . . ." Howard Zinn, "Discovering John Reed," Third World Traveler, http://www.thirdworldtraveler.com/Zinn/John_Reed_HZOH.html (accessed February 26, 2007).

p. 136, "could love and marry and be happy . . ." Rosenstone, *Romantic Revolutionary* , 81.

p. 137, "We have banded together . . ." Ibid., 96.

p. 137-138, "move on . . . If I'm breaking," O'Connor and Walker, *The Lost Revolutionary,* 77.

p. 139, "Two thousand nondescript . . ." Rosenstone, *Romantic Revolutionary*, 153.

p. 140, "the finest reporting . . ." Ibid., 166.

p. 140, "gorgeous panorama" Ibid., 168.

p. 140, "And here are the nations . . ." Zinn, "Discovering John Reed."

p. 140, "not our war," O'Connor and Walker, *The Lost Revolutionary*, 151.

p. 140, "slogging along miles . . ." Ibid., 167.

p. 140, "long, low mounds of earth . . ." Ibid., 105.

p. 141, "War means an ugly mob-madness . . ." Ibid., 265.

p. 141, "Russians themselves are, perhaps . . ." Reed, *Ten Days*, xxviii.

p. 141, "I'm sure I will like..." Rosenstone, *Romantic Revolutionary,* 213.

p. 142, "ripe for revolution," Ibid., 216.

p. 142, "I began to read . . ." Ibid., 9.

p. 143, "an artist, a rampant . . ." Ibid., 239.

p. 143, "the first person . . . " O'Connor and Walker, *The Lost Revolutionary*, 175.

p. 143, "He [the American laborer] will do well . . ." Ibid., 244.

p. 144, "Within a very few months . . ." Ibid., 167.

p. 144, "I must find myself again . . ." Reed, *Ten Days, xxix.*

p. 145, "We are in the middle of things..." Ibid., xxx.

p. 146, "Russian ideas are the most . . ." Rosenstone, *Romantic Revolutionary,* 234.

p. 147, "I love beauty . . ." Ibid., 260.

p. 148, "Now begins a new era . . ." Ibid., 295.

p. 150, "I am a Socialist . . ." Ibid., 317.

p. 150, "I am unable to write . . ." Ibid., 320.

p. 150, "All movements have had somebody . . ." Ibid.

p. 151, "You can't eat your dinner . . ." Ibid., 327.

p. 151, "Knit a Strait-Jacket for Your Soldier Boy" Richard O'Connor and Dale L. Walker (New York: Harcourt, Brace & World, 1967) 193.

p. 153, "I have always advocated . . ." Rosenstone, *Romantic Revolutionary,* 344.

p. 154, "I have nothing to read..." Ibid., 369.

p. 155, "the revolutionary proletariat . . ." Ibid., 376.

p. 156, "On the whole, ideas alone . . ." *Marxist Internet Archive,* "John Reed," http://www.marxists.org/archive/reed/ (accessed February 26, 2007).

p. 156, "All I know is . . ." Ibid., p.4.

Bibliography

Bellamy, Edward. *Looking Backward, 2000-1887.* New York: Penguin Books, 1888.

Brommel, Bernard. *Eugene V. Debs: Spokesman for Labor and Socialism.* Chicago: Charles H. Kerr Publishing Co., 1978.

Curris, Harold. *Eugene V. Debs.* Boston: G.K.Hall & Co, 1976.

Debs, Eugene V. "The Secret of Efficient Expression." *Coming Nation,* July 8, 1911.

Falk, Candace. *Love, Anarchy, and Emma Goldman.* New York: Holt, Rinehart and Winston, 1984.

Fleischmann, Harry. *Norman Thomas: A Biography.* New York: W.W. Norton & Company, Inc., 1964.

Ginger, Ray. *Eugene V. Debs: A Biography.* New York: Collier Books, 1949.

Goldman, Emma. *Living My Life.* 2 vols. New York: Alfred Knopf, Inc., 1931.

Goldman, Emma. *Living My Life.* 2 vols. 1931. Anarchy Archives, 1995. http://dwardmac.pitzer.edu/ANARCHIST_ARCHIVES/goldman/living/living1_11.html.

Harris, Leon. *Upton Sinclair: American Rebel*. New York: Thomas Y. Crowell Company, 1975.

Liukkonen, Petri. "Upton Beall Sinclair." Books and Writers, http://www.kirjasto.sci.fi/sinclair.htm.

Madison, Charles A. *Critics and Crusaders: A Century of American Protest*. New York: Frederick Ungar Publishing Co, 1947.

Marxist Internet Archive. "John Reed." http://www.marxists.org/archive/reed.

Massachusetts Foundation for the Humanities. "Mass Moments: Massachusetts Executes Sacco and Vanzetti. August 23, 1927." http://www.massmoments.org/moment.cfm?mid=245.

O'Connor, Richard and Dale L. Walker. *The Lost Revolutionary*. New York: Harcourt, Brace & World, Inc., 1967.

Reed, John. *Ten Days That Shook the World*. New York: The Modern Library, 1960.

Rosenstone, Robert A. *Romantic Revolutionary*. New York: Vintage Books, 1975.

Salvatore, Nick. *Eugene V. Debs: Citizen and Socialist*. Urbana, IL: University of Illinois Press, 1982.

Seidler, Murray B. *Norman Thomas: Respectable Rebel*. New York: Syracuse University Press, 1961.

Shulman, Alix. *To the Barricades: The Anarchist Life of Emma Goldman*. New York: Thomas Y. Crowell Company, 1971.

Sinclair, Upton. *The Autobiography of Upton Sinclair*. New York: Harcourt, Brace & World, Inc., 1962.

John Simkin's official Web site, "Upton Sinclair." Spartacus Educational, http://www.spartacus.schoolnet.co.uk.

Steward, Dwight. *Mr. Socialism*. New Jersey: Lyle Stuart, Inc., 1974.

Swanberg, W. A. *Norman Thomas: The Last Idealist.* New York: Charles Scribners' Sons, 1976

Thomas, Norman. *Socialism Re-examined.* New York: W.W. Norton & Co., Inc., 1963.

Wexler, Alice. *Emma Goldman: An Intimate Life.* New York: Pantheon Books, 1984.

Yoder, Jon A. *Upton Sinclair.* New York: Frederick Ungar Publishing Co., 1975.

Web sites

http://www.eugenevdebs.com
This comprehensive site details Debs's personal history, his activities as a political activist and union leader, and information about the Debs Foundation. Visitors can take a virtual tour of the Victorian house he built in 1890 for himself and his wife, Kate.

http://sunsite.berkeley.edu/Goldman
This extensive site features the Emma Goldman Papers Project of the University of California at Berkeley. Readers will find a lengthy biographical sketch, a multipage chronology of her life and activities, images, an online exhibit, published essays and personal correspondence, plus a host of other materials by and about Goldman.

http://dwardmac.pitzer.edu/Anarchist_Archives/gold man/ living/livingtoc.html
Emma Goldman's two-volume autobiography *Living My Life* is available to readers on this site, Anarchy Archives, which is maintained by Pitzer College. It also features a biographical sketch, a selection of her writings, photographs, and much more.

http://www.spartacus.schoolnet.co.uk/Jupton.htm
Spartacus Educational provides a biographical sketch of Upton Sinclair on this Web page.

http://sunsite.berkeley.edu/Literature/Sinclair/index.html
The University of California at Berkeley hosts this Web site, which provides an online copy of *The Jungle* as well as study aids for the book. The site also includes a link to letters from Jack London to Upton Sinclair.

http://www.spartacus.schoolnet.co.uk/USAthomas.htm
Spartacus Educational offers a biographical sketch of Thomas as well as a piece written by him that appeared in the *New Republic* on May 26, 1917.

http://www.gutenberg.org/etext/3076
On the Web site of Project Gutenberg readers can download a free copy of *Ten Days that Shook the World* by John Reed.

http://www.marxists.org/archive/reed
On Marxists Online, readers will find the John Reed Internet Archive, which includes articles, letters, and speeches by Reed from 1913 to 1921, as well as a letter written by his wife, Louise Bryant, from Moscow on November 14, 1920. The letter appeared in *The Liberator* in February 1921, and it is titled "The Last Days with John Reed."

Index

DATE DUE

LAKE PARK HIGH SCHOOL
RESOURCE CENTER